THE COMPANY VALUATION PLAYBOOK

Charles Sunnucks

First published in Great Britain in 2021

Design and typesetting by Common Writers

www.commonwriters.com

Paperback ISBN: 978-1-8384708-1-4

Hardback ISBN: 978-1-8384708-2-1

Ebook ISBN: 978-1-8384708-0-7

Contents

For my wife Qi, and two daughters, Isabel and Camilla.

The content of this book stands on the shoulders of many great investors. Investing often gets a bad rap, and it's easy to forget the huge social and economic advances that a more efficient capital market brings. Thanks also to all to those that have lent their time to this book's development, in particular Modwenna Rees-Mogg for her guidance; Katie Ghani, William Sunnucks, Alex Scharzenberger and Geoffrey Elliot for their chapter reviews, plus Helen Castell for her insightful edits.

Foreword

Do stock valuations matter? We know that factors unrelated to valuation can be drivers of returns: themes, narratives and previous returns (momentum) can all dominate market behaviour, sometimes for years. Does this make stock valuations irrelevant, and valuation analysis redundant? For two reasons, I think not.

First, a series of rigorous, empirical studies show that 'value' stocks exhibit higher returns than 'not-value' stocks over the long-term. These studies, by necessity, use simple measures of 'value' for companies, such as the ratio of the net assets of a firm to its market capitalization; or the ratio of share price to reported earnings per share. Such research is numerous and holds up over different time periods and in different markets. Note that this applies over the long-term, not necessarily in the next week or the next three years.

The other reason is more subtle, philosophical even: the price you pay for an asset matters. It *has* to matter. If it didn't matter, what on earth are investment analysts doing? Sure, some analysis is associated with trading: short-term opportunities to profit around private information, or knowledge of the impending or likely trades of some other market participants. But this differs from investing. When investing for the long-term, the price you pay for an asset will determine the ultimate return you receive. And that's why valuation analysis is an important skill and process for an investor.

In this book, Charles Sunnucks leads us in a clear and methodical manner through the steps that an investment analyst is likely to take with an investment opportunity: qualitative perspectives, calculating straight-forward accounting ratios (over time and compared to a peer group) and then on to a discounted cash flow (DCF) analysis.

DCF analysis is the theoretically correct, but not-easy-in-practice, method employed by analysts to estimate the intrinsic value of an asset.

Of special interest in this book are the sections on 'leveraged buyouts' and 'start-ups and early-stage companies' – topics of interest that are too often ignored in finance books. A separate section on the banking sector is included, which is both welcome and appropriate.

This book is not about day-trading, meme stocks or reacting to stock ideas touted on Twitter. That's for someone else to write. This is for those who wish to practice investment analysis as their occupation, whether it be in a professional or personal context. Of course, it's possible to go further still, using reverse-DCF analysis and scenario analysis to understand what assumptions are priced in to current share prices; or to undertake stochastic modelling, specialist sector metrics or more...but ultimately, these rely on the same fundamental principle: that an asset is worth the (estimated) present value of its future cash flows. Combining this with qualitative and accounting analysis, plus risk awareness, this book provides a solid foundation for any aspiring investor.

James Clunie is an Honorary Professor at the University of Edinburgh. Prior to this, he was Head of Global Equities at Aberdeen Asset Management and lead-manager on the long/short Jupiter Absolute Return Fund.

Preface

There are plenty of people with very strong views about what makes a good company, but far fewer who can articulate what makes a good investment. While there are a variety of investment styles an investor might apply, investing over any reasonable period ultimately boils down to a simple reality – if you overpay for a stock you are likely to get stung, and if you underpay then odds are you will profit.

While this principle of buying at the right price is perhaps obvious, and indeed has been extensively written on, far fewer works tackle how to go about this when actually valuing a company. This book is intended to fill the gap between the overly simplified valuation explanations that put you at risk of making costly errors, and heavily academic pieces which lack practical application. It has been borne out of my own frustrating experiences of trying to find informative answers, and I hope it will help the reader avoid a world of pain chasing down hopeless rabbit holes.

The book's content does not focus on fast trading or new-fangled theories. Rather, it introduces you to the simple industry-standard tools used by professionals globally to value companies and their shares. These tools are relevant to all companies, and they range in complexity from those requiring only a pen, paper and calculator right through to the development of a comprehensive Excel discounted cash flow output. While some concepts may appear complicated at first, you only need some basic maths knowledge and a bit of common sense to work through them. As Warren Buffett eloquently put it, "Investing success doesn't correlate with IQ after you're above a score of 25. Once you have ordinary intelligence, then what you need is the temperament to control urges that get others into trouble."

Importantly, taking a fundamental approach to investing will not guarantee you a positive outcome – so do not invest what you cannot afford to lose. It can however help heavily stack the deck in your favour when it comes to making well-informed investment choices, and that in turn can be highly profitable.

Lay of the Land

'Price is what you pay, value is what you get'– Warren Buffett

The legal concept of 'the company' has proven to be one of the most enduring, influential and revolutionary human constructions in the history of civilisation. Whether we consume from one, work at one, or simply benefit from the tax dollars they create, companies are an inextricable part of modern-day life. The tools presented in this book will provide a framework to help you fully understand the forces that drive companies, how to then make robust forward-looking projections about these entities, and finally how to determine the value of their shares.

Valuation methods

There are a number of company valuation methods, the two key ones being relative valuation and intrinsic valuation. Relative valuation is simple and quick but a bit of a blunt tool. Intrinsic valuation has far more academic rigour, but does take more time. Both are well worth understanding and can be used in combination or independently.

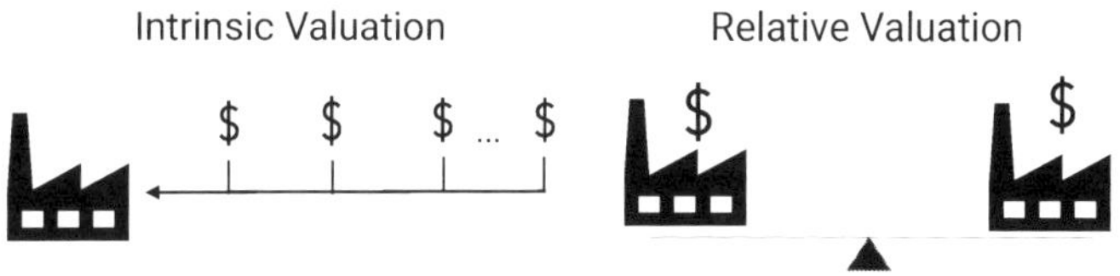

Relative valuation is based on comparative analysis, the principle being that companies with similar return and risk profiles should trade at a similar valuation. The challenge of course is that the scale and profitability of companies can vary substantially. Therefore, rather than comparing companies in terms of dollar values, this method anchors their valuation to a ratio – a multiple or yield. This standardises the valuation and makes it easily comparable across a company's peer group as well as its own history. The most commonly used ratio is the price-to-earnings multiple ('PE'), which is calculated as price divided by earnings.

Importantly, if you are raring to go and simply want a rough-and-ready roadmap for company valuation, skip straight to the chapter on relative valuation.

Intrinsic valuation takes a more absolutist approach. It is founded on the concept that a company's value today is based on the returns it will generate in the future. This is calculated by 'discounting cash flows to a present value' – a term that will need some unpacking later. While the actual valuation itself is relatively quick to complete, an accurate output is normally best reached with the development of a forward-looking financial model, and this can take more time. The intrinsic method of valuation is therefore more frequently used by financial professionals with time to commit than by individual investors.

THE CAPITAL MARKETS

For many individuals, their purpose for valuing a company will be to identify not just what makes a good company, but what makes a good investment. That is, so they can buy if they determine the company is undervalued (fair value higher than price), or sell if it is overvalued (fair value lower than price). Investing then becomes far less of a gamble when informed choices can stack the deck heavily in your favour. This is true for any type of company, no matter its industry or size, quality or growth outlook.

Those that invest are participating in the global capital market – a market that matches those that have money ('capital') with those that want it. For the purpose of company valuation, that capital is transacted in return for a share in the business and the investor becomes a part owner – a 'shareholder' with 'equity'. The more shares you own, the greater your ownership, with percentage ownership proportional to total shares outstanding. So for example, if a company had 100 shares in total and an investor owned three, that investor would own 3% of the company (3 ÷ 100 = 3%).

As a shareholder, you are entitled to profits available for distribution (dividends) and have a claim to the net assets of the business in the event it is wound up or sold. Once shares in a company have been issued, in what is known as a 'primary' market transaction, those shares can then be freely brought or sold independent of the company. Trading in shares subsequent to initial issuance is done in what is commonly known as the secondary market, which is where the vast majority of transactions occur. The relationship between the primary and secondary market can be likened to how a central bank issues bank notes but then has no direct involvement in their subsequent exchange, such as when you use cash to buy a coffee or groceries.

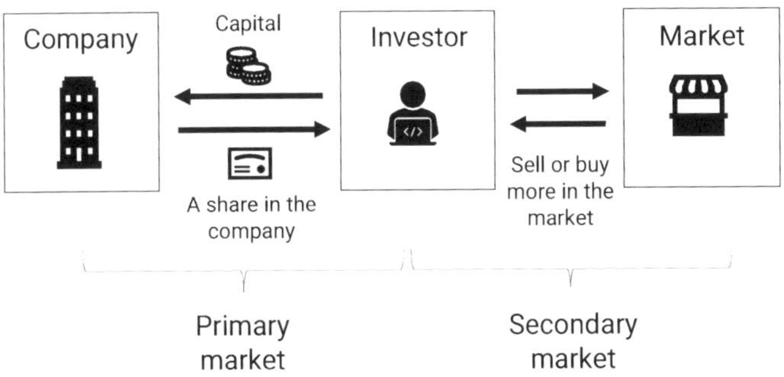

For shares, there are two major market types – the public market and the private market. Publicly listed shares are available to sell and buy on formal exchanges such as those of New York, London or Hong

Kong. When these shares first list on the exchange, that is known as an initial public offering (IPO). After a company lists its shares on a public exchange, transactions can be done seamlessly, whether you are an individual or a professional. Indeed, you could buy and sell shares in a company multiple times in a single day if you wanted to trade aggressively. Details on public companies are readily available online, either through the company's 'investor relations' webpage or online finance sites such as Bloomberg, Google Finance or Yahoo Finance, where charts, key ratios, peers and performance numbers can be pulled for free.

In the private markets meanwhile, the shares of a company are far less readily traded as there is no formal exchange. Private companies are typically less developed and smaller, and not yet in a position to justify the heavy disclosure requirements and significant costs associated with a public listing. Transactions in the private markets are far more cumbersome, often requiring lawyers and investment bankers to seal a deal. But as with public equity, the opportunity to profit from transactions can be considerable.

While investing has certainly been subject to heavy criticism over the years – much of it justified – the act of valuing a company and allocating capital is of significant social good. It means that new or growing businesses can receive enough capital to meet their needs, while also providing a channel for savers to put their money to work. It additionally promotes the democratisation of finance, whereby whether as an individual with $100 or a corporation with $100 million you can become a part owner in a company who is entitled to vote on key decisions and participate in its success.

Beyond the direct benefits of capital market activity, when using a fundamental valuation framework to inform investment decisions, you are providing an important role in price discovery and the efficient allocation of resources across the economy. If the price of apples at a market doubled, farmers would be incentivised to produce more apples, the supply of apples would increase and the price would correct. Likewise, in capital markets, when you effect change in a company's share price by buying or selling shares, that sends a signal to enterprises and entrepreneurs where resources might be most profitability deployed. Over the long term, often this can be a far more powerful influence on corporate decision-making than most government policy or market conditions.

A word of warning...

Techniques learned in this book can be used to value anything from a small start-up to a mature enterprise. Indeed, they will provide a foundation upon which you may value any other financial asset.

I offer them however with three notes of caution:

- Your output will ultimately only be as good as the assumptions driving it. This is why it is not unusual for different individuals to ascribe different valuations to the same company.
- The valuation you develop will be for that point in time only. As new information develops, so too should your outlook – so you must be willing to adapt.
- We are all riddled with behavioural biases that to some extent cloud our objective judgement. These will be detailed later in the book, but essentially, avoid simple errors by taking a clear, consistent, and structured approach when assessing any valuation target.

ASSESS

Qualitative Analysis

'Set your course by the stars, not by the lights of every passing ship' – *General Omar N. Bradley*

So, you have a company you want to value. Perhaps you work for it, founded it, compete against it or just want to invest in it – it matters not. Beauty may be in the eye of the beholder, but valuation isn't. It is an output made entirely independent of your attachment or preferences. However, while the valuation process itself should be objective, assumptions are required to drive the output, and this requires an understanding of the company being valued.

Companies are complex. There are hundreds of variables that dictate each one's outlook and an overwhelming amount of information that an investor could utilise, making analysis a daunting task. Indeed, it is easy to fall victim to 'paralysis from analysis' and to miss the woods for the trees entirely.

Therefore, rather than seeking to incorporate every possible aspect of a company into your analysis, instead strip the company back to the key forces that shape its future and use these as the foundation for future projections.

These forces can be summarised using the Court, Castle & Moat approach.

This approach uses 'Court' as an analogy for management quality, 'Castle' for the strength of a business, and 'Moat' for its defenses against competitive forces.

Under this model, a company that is a strong investment prospect would have a good court that manages an attractive castle that is also well defended by its moat.

While the valuation tools presented in this book can be applied to any asset, good or bad, try and ask yourself early on if a company is really worth valuing. If not, move on.

The Court

In the Middle Ages, each kingdom had a court. This acted as an important decision-making body, helping determine the kingdom's fate. In current times, each company has a senior management team, which similarly has considerable influence over the company's outlook, and therefore its valuation. Good management can turn a bad company around, while bad management can run it into the ground.

There are three key variables that determine how effective a company's top management is likely to be: capability, alignment and accountability. These factors are particularly critical for early-stage investments, when there is little tangible evidence to base an outlook on and management has a considerable role to play in the success or failure of a venture. Even for large mature companies, despite the substantial resources that can be employed to help decision-making, it can be surprising how often bad choices and poor leadership can cripple a company's value. Notably, between 2000 and 2013, it was calculated that about one quarter of Fortune 500 CEO departures were involuntary, demonstrating the extent of poor management performance.

Management capability is one of the easiest of these three variables to analyse and form a view on.

We will focus on the CEO role, but if you have time, the same process can also be used to assess others within the 'c-suite' (chief financial officer, chief investment officer and chief operating officer).

For the CEO, you ultimately want a leader who can build a team that is good at creating long-term value for investors. The most practical way to draw conclusions on the probability of future success in this respect is to have a dig around online for any evidence regarding track record, qualifications and past experience. Be mindful to look beyond the CEO's official biography on the company page and see, for example, if Google News turns up any articles on past activity. If the CEO has in the past managed a public company listed on a stock exchange, you can additionally study historical performance by pulling up the share price and comparing its returns to those of its peers. Looking to see what the share price did on the day the CEO's exit announcement was made often provides the most telling sign. You would normally expect a CEO's departure to create uncertainty and consequently a drop in the share price, so any rise will be a red flag – although this should also be considered in the context of the broader market movement that day.

Senior managers are of course not one dimensional. They are complex beings, with interests and priorities outside of the company, and even the most capable of individuals can quickly inflict damage if not provided with the correct sticks and carrots to create shareholder value. For this reason, it is well worthwhile understanding the processes, procedures and controls that a company has in place to encourage good behaviour. Known as 'corporate governance', this has become increasingly important as the complexity of companies has grown and their ownership become more dispersed.

There are two key elements to corporate governance: management alignment and management accountability. Accountability refers to the extent to which management is accountable to shareholders. This is largely achieved through a shareholder-elected group of individuals who meet regularly and provide management oversight – the board. It is the responsibility of the board to hire the CEO or general manager of the company and assess/determine the overall strategy.

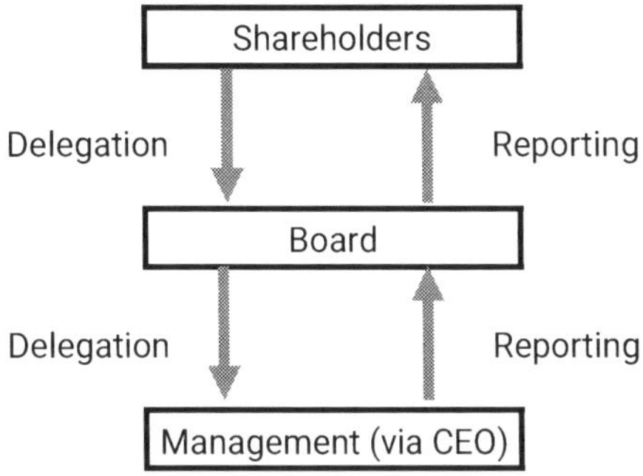

An effective board needs to have the independence, experience and resources necessary to function properly. It should meet regularly outside the presence of management and have the ability to hire external professionals without management approval and to make judgements when required – for example, related to management pay or an acquisition. It is important that board members are also held accountable. Therefore, there should be an opportunity for shareholders to vote on the board members. This is normally done at the annual general meeting and board members often serve on a three-year cycle. As a general rule, at least one third of a listed company's board should be 'independent' of the company or management, and ideally you would expect more than half to be.

As the board is normally decided on by shareholders, if your holding in the company or influence is large enough, you could also gather votes to gain a board seat or directly effect change. This is typically the intention of activist investors, who specifically take a position in a poorly managed company to lobby for shareholder value-enhancing change. For example, this might include selling off parts of the business, taking the company private, paying out more to shareholders, finding efficiencies or voting out bad management. While activist investors have gotten a bad name (as splitting up the business or reducing costs would often lead to redundancies), they are also a valuable market mechanism to keep management accountable and focused on shareholder value. Often, simply the appearance of an activist shareholder on a company's shareholder register can force change even before intervention is made public.

While every company must have at least one director, smaller sized firms may well not be able to justify the expense of having a properly constituted board of directors. In these instances, if the company is not listed, an 'advisory board' is often a substitute. This does not however provide nearly the same level of governance oversight as a formal board, although as the shareholder register of a smaller company is typically more concentrated (fewer investors), direct shareholder scrutiny is in any case more likely.

Alignment is the second measure for assessing how effective a company's corporate governance checks and balances are. While one might hope that a well-paid senior manager would be keen to work for the good of the firm, in practice they are often primarily interested in one stakeholder – themselves. This is known as the 'agency' problem and refers to the conflict of interest that arises between a company's management and shareholders. For example, because executive salaries tend to grow in line with a company's size, and managing a bigger business also brings boasting rights, it is often in a senior manager's interest to use company resources to build business size rather than return cash to shareholders in the form of dividends, even if investments are not value accretive.

While the agency problem cannot be eliminated, it can be minimised. This is normally largely achieved via the structuring of the senior management compensation package – for instance, by linking remuneration to long-term goals and certain KPIs (key performance indicators), rather than simply offering a fixed salary.

This can be particularly effective when remuneration is largely in the form of shares, as this directly aligns management interests with shareholders. If management benefited from ownership, for example, it would likely think twice about embarking on frivolous acquisitions. It is essential however that management shareholder remuneration plans are structured cautiously, as they can create a short-term management mentality. This could manifest as underspending in marketing or research in order to generate higher short-term profits, allowing the manager to possibly exit his or her share plan at an inflated price. It is possible to reduce this risk by ensuring shares can only be sold over multiple years, thereby locking management into a longer-term mindset.

The Castle

Castles in the Middle Ages varied from fabulously grand structures with a prospering community to crumbling ruins plagued with poverty and disease. Likewise, companies come in a variety of conditions, ranging from those simply hoping to survive to those positioned to thrive. For a company, there are four key axes across which we can measure the attractiveness of our castle: its value proposition, its impact on the environment/society, its micro environment and its macro environment.

Before digging deep into a company however, first consider what is the primary factor driving its outlook. Is it specific to the company, the market or the broader economy? This will help you prioritise where you should focus your research efforts. Not every factor is of equal importance, and the order of significance varies between companies. For example, for a pharmaceutical drugs developer, you would likely prioritise understanding the company's value proposition, while for a solar supplier you might prioritise the industry outlook (micro environment), and for a bank, the economic backdrop (macro environment).

Value proposition

A company's value proposition relates to why a customer would choose to purchase its product or service – what makes it competitive. To ascertain this, start by understanding the company's product. Identify what the product or service is, the process to create it, the need that it is fulfilling and the typical profile of the target customer. This sounds like an obvious step, but it is surprisingly often overlooked. For larger companies, most of this information will be but a few clicks away on the internet. For example, if doing research on Heineken, watch its recent YouTube adverts, read customer reviews on brand and taste, pull a company presentation from its website, and investigate how/where their product is produced. Smaller companies will likely require direct engagement with management or a company representative if publicly available information is lacking.

It's not good enough to simply produce a good product or service if others are producing it better on a consistent basis, so seek next to understand the company's competitive strategy. According to Harvard Business School professor Michael Porter, a company can effectively compete using one of two strategies. It can either seek to develop a no-frills cost advantage over its competition or differentiate. Both strategies can be applied at a broad level, across the whole market, or focused on a niche segment.

Source of competitive advantage	Markets where business competes: **Broad**	Markets where business competes: **Narrow**
Costs	Cost Leadership	Cost Focus
Differentiation	Differentiation Leadership	Diversification Focus

If a company opts for a cost leadership strategy, its goal is to have a lower cost structure than its competitors. This edge should then subsequently allow it to either offer a lower price and take market share or retain pricing similar to that of the industry and reap abnormal profits. Cost advantages might be achieved by scale, operational efficiencies, access to a resource or location. This strategy is most often used by companies offering relatively standard products which cannot otherwise easily be differentiated, for example in industries such as manufacturing, mining or farming.

A company can also apply a cost strategy to more complex products or services by being 'cost focused' and targeting a specific sub-segment of the market. It then does not need to offer the lowest price in the market, but simply a lower price than others in that sub-segment. For example, you might be able to purchase a loaf of bread more cheaply at a supermarket, but the local convenience store could compete by being the cheapest within walking distance. The preference in this instance is to be a big fish in a small pond, rather than operate as a small fish in a big pond. It's a particularly common strategy amongst smaller companies that lack broad market appeal and the resources to compete at scale, so instead focus on a niche competitive competence.

A business plan that emphasises differentiation as a strategy is quite different. Here, the company is seeking to create a product or service that is distinctive in terms of quality or delivery. To be successful though, the cost of this differentiation must then be less than the price premium buyers place on the product or service. Great examples of companies that have implemented a successful differentiation strategy include Nike and Apple. As with cost, those that lack broad appeal can specialise in niche industry sub-categories, such as locally brewed beer, organic food or hand-painted crafts. If successful, this strategy can often work as a platform from which to then enter the broader industry.

Environment and social impact considerations

One aspect increasingly being incorporated into the analysis of a company's proposition is the impact its products and processes have on the environment and society. Investors should take an interest in the wider environment and social impacts not just for altruistic reasons. It also makes financial sense to invest in companies which are in tune with all stakeholders, whether they be employees, government bodies, or the wider community in which they operate. These considerations, while commonly referred to as 'externalities', are increasingly being internalised by companies in response to changes in policy and consumer expectations. As a result, the extent to which a company has the proper processes and controls to mitigate, or at least limit, its environmental and social risks is no longer a niche area of company analysis but a very real variable that affects its valuation.

Understanding the environmental and social risks a company is exposed to is complex. Disclosure is often limited, global reporting standards for information are varied, and companies commonly are highly selective in what data they do provide. Even when accurate company information is easily available, we often only get the tip of the iceberg, as the typically complex tangle of supply chains beneath them can yield a variety of risks. Out of sight should not be out of mind however, as these risks can rise up to bite companies if not managed. UK online retailer Boohoo, for example, lost almost half its value in a matter of days following reports in 2020 of poor pay and work conditions within its supply chains.

Environmental factors such as climate change, pollution/waste and the depletion of natural resources create what are known as transition risks and physical risks. Transition risk refers to policy, legal or technology developments which make certain products, processes or activities far costlier or redundant. Reflect for instance on coal-fired power plants and how many have become obsolete due to rising emission standards. Physical risk meanwhile involves the impact that climate change is expected to have in terms of flooding or different weather patterns. These are typically far longer term risks, but are still very much in scope, especially when a company is either in an industry or region likely to be impacted.

Social risks relate to issues such as working conditions, pay ratios and labour standards that are particular to a company. Nike, Amazon and Apple are just a few of the big names that have faced significant issues at some point over poor labour relations within their supply chains. The result was poor publicity and ultimately higher costs as they adjusted to improve. Analysis of this risk however is complicated by what is considered 'good practice'. For instance, an hourly $6 wage in Vietnam would be considered reasonable, whereas the same amount in the UK would be considered highly exploitative. Risks therefore need to be considered in the context of companies' operating environments, as well as their materiality and the actions management has taken to reduce them.

Social risks also extend to factors that affect the company's external stakeholders, such as local communities, tax payers and customers. A cigarette or alcohol brand may, for example, be a good employer, but nonetheless create health and wellness issues for the end consumer – a characteristic which in turn makes these companies vulnerable to policy challenges.

Macro environment

The title to one of English poet John Donne's most famous verses – 'No man is an island' – could just as easily refer to a company. So ask yourself whether the castle you are researching is located in a remote, baron, arctic tundra or in a warm region, teeming with life and energy. The answer will invariably affect how 'attractive' you can consider the castle's prospects to be.

First let's consider the kingdom – the company's macro environment or wider economy. An economy can go through intense periods of feast or famine, swinging through business cycles, with investors flip-flopping between greed and fear. A company that is highly influenced by the business cycle is said to be 'cyclical', while one that operates more independently of its macro backdrop is referred to as a 'non-cyclical'.

There is however no absolute distinction between cyclical and non-cyclical in the case of companies or industries. Rather, they will likely sit somewhere between the two extremes. The distinction is important, not necessarily because it will meaningfully affect our long-term outlook for the company, but, as we will learn in a later chapter, because it will influence how we quantify its risk profile. While no two companies will operate in exactly the same way, we can use the following broad industry classifications to identify how cyclical a company will likely be.

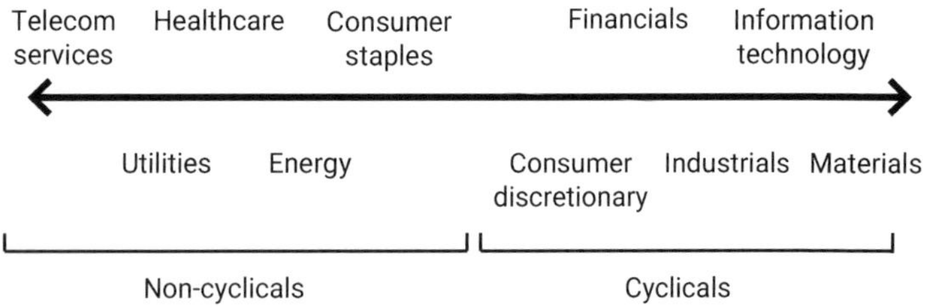

If you are assessing a highly cyclical company during an extreme period, step back, look at its return profile over time and the extent to which it has currently deviated from that, then assess if/when there will be mean reversion to the average. For context, since 1900 a recession has occurred on average roughly every four years, although expansions have been lasting much longer since 1980, and indeed, the current one in the US is the longest on record. Meanwhile, recessions, defined as two consecutive quarters of contracting GDP, last less than a year on average, and subsequent rebounds can often be swift as the economy rebalances. Remember, we are seeking to value the company based on its adjusted cash flows to shareholders into perpetuity, and therefore a dud quarter or even year is really not going to have a severe impact on the end output.

Micro environment

Of typically greater importance to a castle is its immediate region – its micro environment. There are two key elements to industry analysis: the rate of industry growth and the competitive landscape. Professionals will often use projections from consultants or research firms, but if you do not have access to such data, have a look online – industry outlook numbers and commentary are typically not hard to come by.

Industry growth data can be used as a sense check for companies' sales growth projections. However, it can also be utilised to develop a sales forecast. This is done by first inputting the market outlook projection, plus creating market share estimates for the company. The market outlook figure can then be multiplied by the market share estimate to derive a forward-looking company sales figure. As a simple example, if a product was launched and anticipated within a year to take 10% of a $1,000,000 market, then the one-year forward sales assumption would be that sales were $100,000 ($1,000,000 × 10% = $100,000). If in year two the market was assumed to stay flat but with market share rising to 20%, the year two sales forecast would then be $200,000 ($1,000,000 × 20% = $200,000), and so on. This method of sales projection is particularly practical for early-stage companies, where developing an outlook from the bottom up can be problematic.

Operating in a high-growth market is of course a strength. However, that is only one part of industry analysis, as the attractiveness of an industry is also influenced by the extent of its competitive intensity. A framework called 'Porter's five forces' is the most broadly used methodology to assess this, as it captures the characteristics that shape industry outcomes over time.

The weaker the forces collectively, the more attractive the long-term outlook for the industry. So, an ideal industry would be one where there is low existing competitive rivalry, a low threat of new entrants, low threat of substitute products, and low bargaining power of either suppliers or customers. These forces need to be particularly considered when an industry is in the early growth stage and the full force of competitive intensity has yet to develop. Take solar energy for example. When solar became a viable means of creating energy, high demand for silicon gave early players lofty margins and excessive valuations. However, as the industry started to settle down and growth decelerated due to the easy access of new entrants and limited bargaining power of existing names, the product became a commodity. Pricing collapsed, and with it margins, profitability and ultimately company valuations. An assessment using Porter's five forces would have enabled the identification of competition risk before it had happened and the early avoidance of value miscalculation.

The Moat

By now, you will have a firm idea of how well managed and attractive your castle is. Great. Unfortunately, however, as any 11th century lord would tell you, the more attractive the castle, the greater the threat that it will be attacked and looted. For this reason, a moat was a regular feature of most castles. Likewise with a company, if a business is attractive, it will in turn attract competition. Therefore, understanding the breadth and depth of its economic moat provides an insight into the durability of its profitability.

The concept of an economic moat has been embraced by many financial analysts as a key aspect of a company's return profile. Most notably, it has been articulated for decades by Warren Buffett in his annual note to shareholders. In 2020, for example, he wrote:

'So we think in terms of that moat and the ability to keep its width and its impossibility of being crossed as the primary criterion of a great business. And we tell our managers we want the moat widened every year. That doesn't necessarily mean the profit will be more this year than it was last year because it won't be sometimes. However, if the moat is widened every year, the business will do very well. When we see a moat that's tenuous in any way – it's just too risky. We don't know how to evaluate that. And, therefore, we leave it alone. We think that all of our businesses – or virtually all of our businesses – have pretty darned good moats.'

Ultimately, the greater the moat, the greater the confidence in the company's long-term outlook will be. By extension, the lower the risk will be and the higher the valuation. There are a number of economic moats a company might enjoy – and indeed, some benefit from several. The most frequent examples of an economic moat are covered below, although in practice any feature that meaningfully limits replication of a company's success is going to act as a barrier for any prospective entrant.

Switching costs

High switching costs – meaning it is either expensive, a hassle or both to be disconnected from a company's product – represent the most controversial of economic moats. Ask yourself when you last changed your personal email. Probably not in the last decade, as in doing so you would lose a trove of historic emails and your own email address. Similarly, for all the complaints about Facebook's data privacy breaches, do most people switch? No, as doing so would mean losing years of contacts, posts and pictures. Switching costs are therefore superb for the companies that benefit from them, but a real headache for their customers.

For the same reason, however, this moat is also the most liable to regulatory intrusion. Take the telecom industry, for example. In the early days of mobile phones, if you changed operator, you also had to change number. This created a considerable switching cost, which allowed telecom companies to charge inflated prices for mobile plans while also reducing their incentive to treat existing customers well. In short, telecom companies enjoyed a wide moat – at the expense of the consumer. The regulator therefore stepped in and required that all networks allow number portability. This allowed individuals to change telecom company while retaining their phone number. So just like that, the companies' moats were gone and their profitability suffered.

For this reason, if switching costs are your castle's primary form of defense, be sure to understand the regulatory backdrop and whether there is either the political will or capability to implement policy change that might impact upon its advantage.

Low production

Low production costs represent the second economic moat. Cost as a strategic advantage has already been covered, but for it to be an enduring advantage the company needs to credibly demonstrate that it cannot easily be knocked off its perch. The example Warren Buffett often gives when talking about pricing advantage is GEICO, an insurance company that undercuts competitors on price by marketing direct to customers, rather than paying insurance brokers. Another example often cited is the sustained cost advantage enjoyed by some commodity producers. For example, Saudi Aramco is the largest oil producer in the world and – if you believe the stock market – also one of the world's most valuable companies. Its oil production costs are considerably below the global average, giving it a sustainable cost advantage over competitors in this area. Having this moat means that not only does the company generate big profits when oil prices are high, but that its prospects remain good even when oil prices plummet. This is because it can afford to keep pumping at oil prices that would generate a loss for its competitors, allowing it to build market share when rivals are forced to stop investing or even exit the market.

Network – marketplace, data, platform

In the 20th century, many of the most valuable companies – for example, big supermarkets, railroads and refiners – were able to sustain a competitive advantage due to economies of scale or intangible moats such as government contracts. Increasingly however, the most durable moats are based on network effects. A network effect is said to occur when a product or service offers more value to the user the more it is used. For example, the telephone would not have been a relevant product had the pool of buyers been limited to a handful of households. However, scale begot scale, success bred further success, and growth quickly compounded to make it for decades an almost ubiquitously owned product across households.

Nowadays, the network effect can be split into three main types: the data network, marketplace network and platform network. The data network is arguably the most considerable, and it is particularly relevant to online companies, where data is becoming one of the most formidable moats of the future. Take Google, for example. The more we use it, the smarter its algorithms become at anticipating what we are searching for. That improves our user experience, so we use it more.

Microsoft, one of the largest companies on this planet, has tried to attack Google's particularly attractive castle with Bing. However, it has been left flailing far behind in second place due to a fatal loop of poor user experience, which is driven by a lack of user data, which results in fewer users, and so on...

The second type of network effect, the marketplace network, is nothing new. Before the days of large retailers, shopping was done at physical markets – places where buyers and sellers could meet to transact goods for cash. The more sellers that set up stall there, the more buyers that would be attracted to shopping there, and so on. Similarly, when you buy or sell a publicly listed equity, that is done via the stock exchange – a market for investors to transact. Beyond the regulatory hurdles, if I wanted to compete with the London Stock Exchange, it would be extremely difficult to attract buyers and sellers to agree at enough scale to convene at a new exchange. As a consequence, existing exchanges that benefit from the moat that the network effect creates are often listed, highly profitable and durable companies.

More recently, marketplace network effects have been developed online. Ebay and Amazon have created substantial economic moats by developing a central online marketplace for buyers and sellers. Uber has created a marketplace matching passengers and drivers on an app and Airbnb succeeded with a marketplace matching those wanting to rent out their home with those seeking accommodation. In these cases, investors have been willing to endure years of multi-million-dollar losses while they wait for the company to dig out an enduring marketplace moat to protect against future competition.

The third and final network effect is the platform effect that occurs when a company is able to keep its customers engaged in its ecosystem and create a sticky user base. For example, if you buy an Apple iPhone, you will probably also spend on the iPhone app store, purchase Apple cloud storage space or buy an Apple computer so that you can synchronise your devices. For a properly integrated Apple user, unscrambling oneself from the Apple ecosystem would be a big hassle, while remaining within it adds convenience. This has allowed Apple to price at a premium, while seamlessly introducing new products and services to already engaged users.

Intellectual property

Intangible assets are company assets without physical substance – namely, brands and intellectual property (copyrights/patents). Coca-Cola and Nike, for example, literally spend billions digging a deep brand moat to build on and protect their prospects. This allows them to maintain the ability to price at a premium to their competition and retain control of an attractive castle. Remember however, while a moat protects, it does not make the castle impregnable. Brands that do not keep up with the times can become defunct, with the root cause typically being bad management, an unwillingness to maintain the moat with ongoing investment, or a reluctance to adapt and recognise change. Consider, for example, Fila. In the 1980s, Fila enjoyed a period as the second-largest basketball shoe retailer in the world, and by 1996 it had become the third-largest athletic shoe retailer in the world. Yet now, in most countries, its brand presence has diminished to at most a couple of retro retail shops.

The second type of intangible asset, intellectual property (IP), is one of the more legally defined economic moats. Patents, for instance, protect inventions or discoveries, be they for pharmaceuticals, tools or software. These grant the company an effective monopoly on that particular product or good, achieving this without all the regulatory inconveniences that might otherwise affect the company's ability to set a price. The purpose of the IP system is to try and strike the right balance between encouraging investment in new, innovative products and ensuring that society benefits from advances by limiting a patent's 'life', typically to around 20 years. Once a patent expires, other companies can legally replicate the product, at which point pricing usually collapses and revenue declines sharply – known as the 'patent cliff'. This can be a particular issue for pharmaceutical companies when patent expiry looms for one or more of the mere handful of drugs they often generate most of their profits from.

Efficient scale advantage

An efficient scale advantage occurs when a company is able to maintain a leading position because the size of its operations deters upstarts, or because of a combination of limited demand and geographic dominance. For example, if there is already a train line between two major cities, the incumbent train operator could be described as having an efficient scale advantage. This is because it would be highly unlikely for a newcomer to attempt to develop an additional line along the same route. Demand would at best only rise slightly, meaning the economics would simply not stack up.

Because of the nature of efficient scale advantage, businesses that benefit from it have usually been established for some time. They also often operate in what is referred to as a natural monopoly, and so are nearly always regulated to ensure they do not disadvantage consumers with excessively high prices or poor service. Indeed, these businesses often live with the constant threat of nationalisation from those that advocate a greater role for the state in an economy – be it healthcare in the US, train services in the UK or public utilities in any number of countries. Despite this, these companies normally have a fairly limited risk profile, as one can project with relative confidence what their cash flow outlook will look like. As a result, they are usually not particularly cyclical.

Summary

Companies are complex, but analysis of them need not be, as long as a structured approach is followed to identify the key forces that shape their outlook. This can be achieved using the Court, Castle & Moat approach, an allegorical method which strips back the process to its basics, providing a proper foundation from which to forecast. As analogies, the 'court' signifies a company's senior management, the 'castle' corresponds to its business strengths, and the 'moat' symbolises a firm's ability to protect its prospects from competition.

Quantitative Analysis

'Accounting is the language of business' – Warren Buffett

Financial analysis is where the rubber meets the road in terms of insight into a company's actual performance. Here, we strip back the layers of glossy management narrative and peer under the hood to see what in practice have been the experienced operational outcomes of the company and the state of its financial health. These statements will then form the foundation of a forward outlook.

Listed companies are required every three to six months to publicly issue financial statements, which are typically accompanied by a management conference call so that any questions can be answered. The statements can be found on the company's website.

For private companies, limited statutory information is available on public registers, but as these companies do not sell shares to the general public, there is no legal requirement to publicly disclose full results. Unless management is willing to do so, it can be difficult to conduct thorough analysis of such firms.

The financial statements of a company are split into three separate sections: the balance sheet, the income statement and the cash flow statement. Although these statements are interconnected, and should all be assessed collectively, they each detail a different aspect of a company's position/performance.

- The balance sheet, sometimes known as the 'statement of financial position', provides a static snapshot of a firm's financial position – what it owns (assets), owes (liabilities) and money attributable to its owners (shareholder equity).

- The income statement is a performance report that matches costs with sales.
- The cash flow statement is a performance report based on cash inflows/outflows.

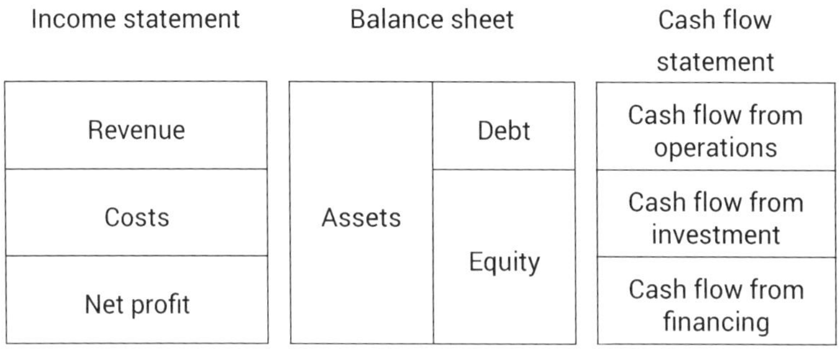

Importantly, management cannot simply decide for itself what to disclose or how to disclose it. There are accounting standards that must be followed. In addition, while management might prepare the financial statements, an independent third-party auditor is required to assess the accuracy of results and their compliance with accounting standards.

Globally, financial accounting standards between different regulators are very similar, although there are distinctions. The two key standards are GAAP (generally accepted accounting principles) and IFRS (international financial reporting standards). Over 140 countries globally have adopted IFRS, while GAAP is largely only used by companies based or listed in the US.

For a high-level understanding of financial statements, the differences are very minor. Ultimately, both seek to ensure company reports are transparent, comprehensive and consistent. As a general observation though, IFRS leaves greater scope for interpretation, whereas

GAAP is more rules based. For the purpose of the overview below, the accounting statement deviations are not materially relevant.

Income statement

The income statement is the primary financial statement that is referred to when analysts talk about performance. It is based on accrual accounting, rather than cash-based transactions – the distinction being that rather than recognising revenue and costs when they are received or paid, they are instead recognised when earned or incurred. For example, imagine buying a piano in a deal that requires no payment for the first six months. From the seller's perspective, a piano has been sold, but no cash has been received yet. In that company's cash flow statement, therefore, no sale would appear for the time being. However, the sale would be immediately recognised in its income statement on the very day you wheeled your piano off its shop floor.

Recognise the sale in the income statement upon sale of the piano

Recognise a cash inflow in the cash flow statement upon receipt of cash

Transaction timing differences probably feel minor in the context of our own everyday dealings (grocery shopping, etc). But for a company, they can substantially alter the shape and outcome of results when applied to both costs and revenue. The consequence is that performance becomes less lumpy, and more grounded in economic reality.

Accounting standards set out to make the structure of income statements consistent across all companies. At a high level, they ensure items are presented in the same order: sales (revenue) minus costs equals net income (profit). Most items on the income statement should be relatively self-explanatory. However, some do need clarification:

Revenue	The sale of a product or service
Costs	Direct costs
Gross profit	**Revenue minus costs**
Marketing	Indirect costs
Research & Development	Indirect cost
General & Administrative	Indirect costs
Operating profit	**Gross profit minus expenses**
Interest	The cost of debt financing
Earnings before tax	**Operating profit minus interest**
Tax	Amount owed in tax
Net income	**Earnings before tax minus tax**

Revenue, appearing on the first line of the income statement, refers to the amount reported from the sale of goods and services in the normal course of business. It is recognised only when the risk and reward of ownership is transferred, and when revenue and cost can be reliably measured. In the majority of cases, it is very clear when recognition should take place, although it becomes more complex when a sale takes place over multiple reporting periods – for example, if a building developer has pre-sold but not completed a development. In these cases, an approach called the 'percentage of completion' method is sometimes applied, whereby only the portion completed is recognised in the income statement. In the example of the developer, if 20% of the development was sold in a financial quarter, then 20% of the sales price would be recognised in the income statement for that period.

The next stage is recognising costs. For accounting purposes, these are divided into direct and non-direct costs. Direct costs are costs that are directly involved in the actual production of the good or service, and are matched to revenue. Indirect costs are typically fixed overhead expenses that are general to the firm, and are expensed in the period incurred.

Direct costs	Indirect costs
Direct labour	Rent
Direct materials	Utilities
Manufacturing supplies	General office expenses
Equipment	Marketing campaigns

For direct costs, most items can clearly be categorised and matched with sales. In our earlier piano example, the company selling the piano would, at the same time as recognising revenue, also recognise the amount that it spent to procure the piano for sale in the first place. This irons out some of the performance creases that would otherwise occur if there was a timing difference between when inventory was purchased or produced, and when it was sold.

What happens when the benefit of a direct cost cannot be matched to any single sale, but is derived over multiple years? For example, imagine an airline company that purchases an airplane to transport paying customers, or a manufacturer that acquires a machine to produce goods. In such cases, it is clearly impractical to recognise the cost in a single period, as this would not appropriately match the cost with its use. Accountants therefore 'capitalise' the cost. Capitalising a cost means that rather than putting it through the income statement straight away, it is instead considered a long-term asset and the cost is then spread over its useful life. If the capitalised asset is tangible (for example, equipment), we call the cost 'depreciation'. If it is non-tangible (such as a patent), we call it 'amortised'.

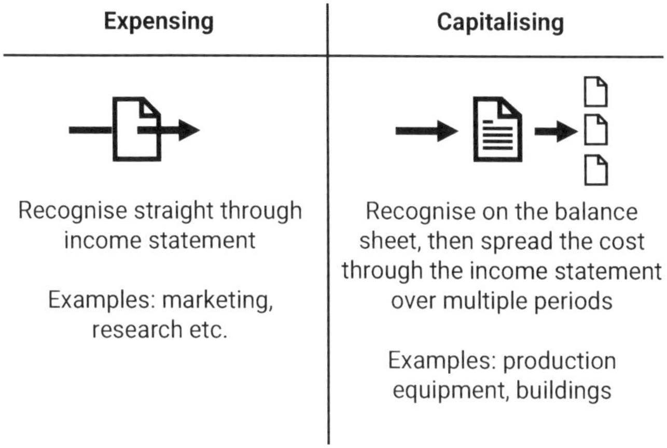

There are a number of ways that a company can recognise depreciation or amortisation, the most commonly used of which is the 'straight line' method. This involves estimating the capitalised asset's end-of-life salvage value and then subtracting this from its original value to derive a net cost. The net cost of the asset is then divided by the asset's useful life, to equal the annual depreciation/amortisation cost charged over the life of that asset in the income statement.

This might sound complex, but in practice we treat many large purchases in a similar way. For example, if you bought a car for \$10,000 and received \$200 when you sold it for scrap 20 years later, you could rationalise that the annual cost of owning that car was effectively \$490 (\$9,800 ÷ 20).

	2021	**2022**	**2023**	**2024**

Depreciation of the asset	-$490	-$490	-$490	-$490...
Expensing the cost	-$9,800			

Other measures of depreciation include accelerated depreciation methods that recognise proportionally more in the early years of use. These are more complex methods that are less commonly applied but arguably better tie depreciation to economic value. For example, when we purchase a car, the biggest decline in its value occurs in the early days and months of use, with a much smaller change in value occurring between years 10 and 20. Application of the accelerated depreciation model results in higher costs and lower profits in the early stages of an asset's use, but lower costs and higher profits in the latter years of use.

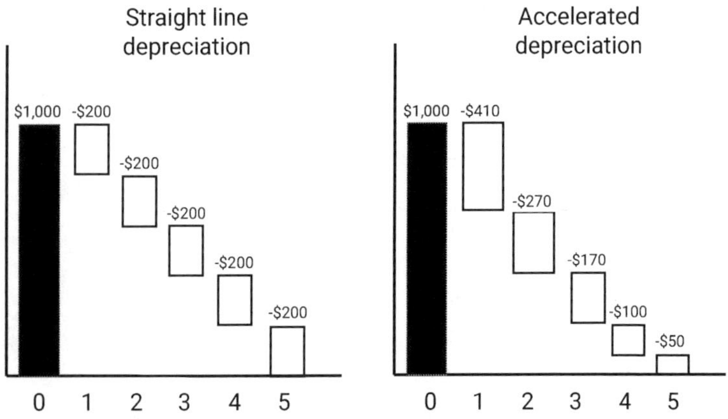

Revenue minus direct costs equals gross profit – a summary measure of profitability. For the purpose of analysis, we can transform it into a standardised figure by calculating it as a percentage of sales – gross profit divided by sales. This derives the gross profit margin, a far more descriptive figure that can be compared across time and peers. For example, if a company has a gross profit of 60% and its peers have one of 50%, it would be reasonable to explore why there is that difference, whether it has always been the case, and if it can persist being so in the future. The gross profit margin also allows us to develop a gross profit projection based on projected sales. For example, if the company's gross margin is stable at 60% and we expect $1 billion of sales next year, we can reason that this will likely equate to $600 million of gross profit ($1bn x 0.6) in the forward year.

Indirect costs make up the other key cost category. These include costs that are not directly attached to the production of a good or service – items such as marketing, administration, distribution and research. Rather than trying to match these costs with sales, they are expensed in the period incurred.

While indirect costs may not be directly associated with a sale, neither are they typically entirely independent. For example, a marketing campaign will likely drum up more sales than if no promotion had been made. The extent to which indirect costs are correlated with revenue will be an important consideration when we come to projecting these items forward and when judging a company's operating leverage. Clues regarding the correlation can often be found by assessing the company's culture and strategy. For example, is management remuneration results based or a fixed amount? Does the company seek to proportionally reinvest profits in research or is that a fixed budget? Is marketing based on brand or performance?

Subtracting indirect costs from gross profit gives operating profit – another summary measure of profitability. As with gross profit, this is best calculated as a percentage of sales to standardise it for comparative purposes. This is known as the operating profit margin, or 'EBIT margin' (earnings before interest and tax). Relative to the gross margin, the operating profit margin is a less raw measure of product/service level profitability, but is more inclusive in so far as it reflects all operating costs. Again, compare this over time and against peers to discern any trends or anomalies.

Beyond key operational performance, a company may have other sources of income or costs which are not directly related to the firm's core operations. These are labelled non-operating income and might, for example, include asset write-downs or gains/losses from foreign exchange. As these are typically one-off and very hard to predict, you may want to consider adjusting results to exclude these items when analysing past trends.

Other than a company's operating activity, its debt financing activity must also be costed. Debt for a firm takes various forms, including loans, bonds, lines of credit and convertible debt. While the structures and cash flow timing may vary dependent on the bond terms, for the purpose of the income statement, the amount recognised is roughly equal to the outstanding principal amount on the balance sheet multiplied by its effective interest rate. This avoids large or lumpy one-off expenses.

The cost of debt on the income statement is known as 'interest expense'. This is a fixed cost to the business and creates increased volatility in earnings. It will benefit shareholders if operating profits rise, but can be disastrous in the event that interest cannot be paid from operating profits (EBIT). For this reason, interest payments are scrutinised using the interest cover ratio: EBIT divided by interest.

The interest cover ratio is a helpful risk measure, as it quantifies how easily a firm is able to meet its interest obligation. What is a reasonable coverage level varies greatly between industries, but certainly anything consistently close to a ratio of one (1) would suggest that the company is at risk of not being able to make payments. This is dangerous, as if a company cannot meet its debt obligations, debt holders have a right to liquidate the business in order to receive repayment. Bear in mind however, that operating cash profits can vary significantly from accrual equivalents, and therefore just because a company cannot pay in in one period does not mean that it is breaching its debt obligations. In addition, a company can draw on cash reserves, additional debt funding or equity issuance to meet repayments if it is operationally under pressure.

The final cost is to the taxman. Just like people, corporations must pay tax, and the amount paid varies between geographies. It is also liable to change over time, for instance the corporate income tax rate in the UK dropped from 30% in 2000 to 19% in 2017, and will rise to 25% in 2023. Current country level corporate tax rates at the time of writing are provided below.

Country	**Tax rate**
United States	27%
United Kingdom	19%
Japan	31%
Germany	30%
Hong Kong	17%
France	28%

We can calculate a firm's 'effective tax rate' by dividing its tax cost by its EBIT. The effective tax rate should be compared against the corporate tax rate for the country it operates in and, if it differs materially, we should seek to understand why. Most countries have tax exemptions, tax holidays, etc. These can be long or short term in nature, making a difference to the company's future profitability. Larger firms will often go to great lengths to reduce their tax bill, for example by incorporating the company or certain parts of it in a low tax domicile such as the Cayman Islands. Tax avoidance is legal, but tax evasion (withholding information from the authorities, etc) is illegal.

To calculate net income, otherwise known as profit after tax, profit or net profit, we add together operating and other income, then subtract tax expense. This is otherwise known as net profit or the 'bottom line' and is typically the single most analysed number within a firm's financial statements, as it sums up all prior revenue and costs. Notably, net income will almost certainly never align to cash profits, due to all the adjustments made to match sales with costs. So do not assume that simply because the company is net income profitable, it is as a whole generating cash.

While net income represents the 'bottom line' for most companies, sometimes businesses will also include a line for 'minority interest' or 'other comprehensive income' in their financial statement. In the case of minority interests, this is required when the company has majority ownership, but not total ownership, of another company (known as a subsidiary). In this instance, the financial statements of the subsidiary are entirely consolidated into the company's financial statements. In order to then account for the portion of net income from the subsidiary not due to the company, a minority interest line is introduced, and the percentage of net income owed to the minority investors in the subsidiary is added together. There is then a final 'net income to shareholders of the company' line below, which subtracts that minority interest figure from net income to derive the total net amount that equity holders of the company are entitled to. In this instance, the 'net income to shareholders' line becomes the 'bottom' line, and most relevant figure for overall analysis of profitability.

Sales	$200
Costs	$150
Profit before tax	$50
Tax	$10
Profit	$40
Minority Interest	$5
Profit attributable to shareholders	$35

The subsidairies minority shareholders

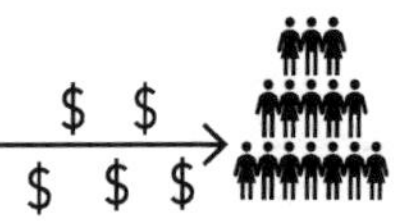

In the case of 'other comprehensive income', this is often a relatively minor figure in the context of company performance, and is not typically used when assessing overall activity/trends. Outside of dividend distributions to shareholders (covered later), it includes all variables that affect a company's retained earnings outside of net income. This will include adjustments like foreign currency translation gains/losses, pension liability adjustments and unrealised gains from securities that are available for sale. Due to the highly uncertain nature of this line, it is normally forecast to be zero in future periods. If it is persistently a meaningful number in the context of company operations, we should seek to understand why that is and whether it is liable to change.

Balance sheet

The balance sheet is a static snapshot of the company's assets (what it owns), liabilities (what it owes) and equity (shareholder ownership). The key principle with regards to a balance sheet is that it must 'balance' – assets on the one side, liabilities and equity on the other.

This principle can be mathematically illustrated as 'Assets = Debt + Equity'. This is a very important relationship, and from it we can derive the balance sheet value of equity by subtracting liabilities from assets. Consider, for example, a house worth $500,000, purchased with a mortgage outstanding of $300,000. In this example, the house would be the 'asset' and the mortgage the 'liability', while the $200,000 left after the mortgage has been subtracted from the property value would be the owner's equity. In practice, for a company, the equity value within the balance sheet – known as equity book value – is by no means a perfect approximation of underlying actual value, but it is a helpful starting point.

The balance sheet is structured starting with assets, then liabilities, and finally equity. Equity and liabilities are broken out between 'current' and 'non-current' Below is a simple example of what items you might expect to see included on one.

Assets	
Current assets	
Cash	Converted to cash within a year
Receivables	
Non-current assets	
Property, plant & equipment (PP&E)	Full value not realised in a single accounting year
Goodwill	
Liabilities	
Current liabilities	
Payables	Obligations due within a year
Deferred tax	
Non-current liabilities	Obligations due in more than one year
Debt	
Equity	
Retained earnings	What a shareholder owns
Contributed capital	

'Assets' is an extremely broad term, in theory capturing everything the company owns. For the purpose of accounting, assets are split into two types: current assets and non-current assets. Current assets are liquid assets that can be easily converted into cash or used up within one year. Groupings include cash and cash equivalents, and marketable securities (highly liquid investments). Non-current assets, however, are less liquid and used over multiple years (equipment, land, etc).

Within current assets, the groupings used can vary from company to company. There are two types of current asset, however, that are particularly important to understand properly: receivables and inventory. Receivables relate to sales made by a company, but for which payment has not yet been received. Inventory relates to products that a company has made or bought with the intention of selling, but which have not yet been sold. These assets therefore arise as a consequence of the accrual adjustments made in the income statement. Both sit on the balance sheet until either cash is collected (in the case of receivables) or the product has been sold (in the case of inventory). At this point, the receivable/inventory balance declines and the balance sheet cash position increases by an equivalent amount.

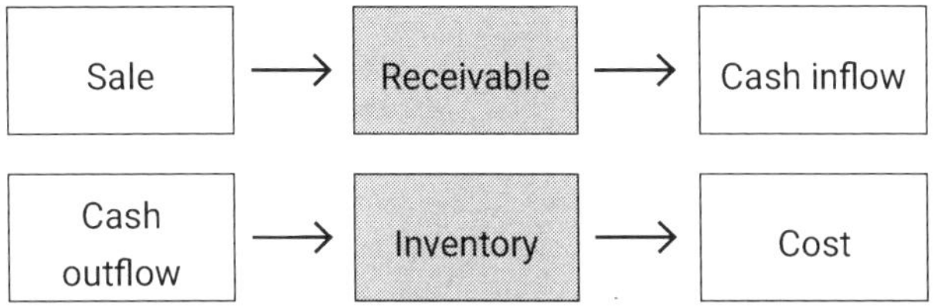

Within non-current assets, property, plant and equipment (PP&E) is typically the major line item. As explained, these are capitalised costs which, rather than being expensed in the period purchased, sit on the balance sheet and depreciate/amortise over their useful life. These are typically recognised as a single item: net PP&E. Net PP&E is calculated as the historical cost of the asset (including delivery/installation) minus accumulated depreciation or amortisation. Therefore, as time goes by, in the very unlikely event that there was no further investment by a company, the PP&E balance would gradually decline to zero.

	2021	2022	2023	2024
PP&E historical cost	$800	$800	$800	$800

Depreciation charge	$200	$200	$200	$200
Net PP&E	$600	$400	$200	$0

While you would normally expect the balance sheet value of PP&E to be a reasonably fair reflection of the economic benefits that the company will derive from it, the accounting value and actual value can sometimes decouple over time. In the event that the value of the asset rises above its balance sheet value, no adjustment is made. However, in the case that its balance sheet value is considered meaningfully overstated, an 'impairment' is recognised to reflect the difference. Any impairment charges for PP&E are included in the 'other income' line described in the income statement section, and for analytical purposes are treated as one-off.

Non-current assets might sometimes also include intangible assets. These are assets that lack physical substance, and can comprise, for example, copyrights, patents, franchises, trademarks and goodwill. Notably however, intangible assets are almost exclusively only recognised as the result of a purchase. For example, if a company purchased a patent for $100,000, that would be its starting balance sheet value within intangible assets. What a company cannot do, other than in a limited number of circumstances, is generate an intangible asset internally. For example, if a patent had been developed by a company, resources that had gone into that process would have been expensed in the period incurred as a R&D (research and development) cost. As a result, for many companies the most valuable part of their business – brand value – is not incorporated on the balance sheet at all. While this reduces subjectivity in accounting standards, thereby limiting the scope for results manipulation, it also nearly always results in an understated book value for the company in question. This is why many companies have a market value that is several times bigger than their equity book value.

The one intangible asset that is not amortised over the period of its useful life is goodwill. Goodwill is only created in a purchase acquisition and is calculated as the purchase price of the acquired company minus its book value. For example, if a company was purchased by another company for $10 million but only had an equity book value of $7 million, the balance sheets of the two companies would be consolidated and the remaining $3 million become a goodwill item in non-current assets.

Goodwill = acquisition price – equity book value

$3 million = $10 million – $7 million

While the name suggests that the acquirer has paid the additional amount above balance sheet value out of 'goodwill', in practice the value of goodwill will in effect be roughly equivalent to the value of off-balance sheet assets such as brand value, client lists, technology, etc.

While goodwill may not be amortised, it is tested for impairment at least annually. If found impaired, (its balance sheet carrying value greater than its actual value), goodwill is reduced and the loss is recognised in the income statement. As long as goodwill is not impaired, it can remain on the balance sheet indefinitely, with no 'cost' recognised in the income statement. For this reason, when one firm buys another, the buying company's management is sometimes guilty of trying to manipulate near-term future net income upward by allocating more of the acquisition price to goodwill (not amortised) and less to identifiable assets (depreciated/amortised).

If assets are what a company owns, then liabilities are what it owes. The term 'liabilities' is intentionally broad, incorporating all present obligations that have arisen from past events. Like assets, liabilities are split into two sections: current (obligations satisfied in one year) and non-current (obligations due in more than one year). Typically, current liabilities will include items such as payables, deferred tax and deferred revenue, while non-current liabilities are commonly dominated by company debt.

Within current liabilities, as with assets, groupings may vary between companies, but it is generally obvious from their name what they cover. One more complex item is trade payables – the amount due to vendors for the supply of inventory. It is a working capital item, just like inventory or receivables, but represents an outflow of economic benefits rather than an inflow (hence its appearance as a liability rather than an asset).

While companies that provide everyday services or products to individuals will unlikely give payable terms in practice, businesses selling to other companies often do, such as when Siemens sells equipment to power stations. Cash flow management is an important aspect of a company's operations, and being able to delay payment can ease cash flow pressures.

Deferred taxes are another common feature of current liabilities, although they can also be a non-current liability or even an asset. They represent the difference between tax paid on the income statement and taxes due (or in the case of a tax asset, paid in advance). The difference most often arises due to disparities between accounting standards and the approach required by tax authorities – such as in companies' depreciation expense treatment. For example, companies will normally use a straight line in their accounted results, but often prefer to apply accelerated depreciation for tax purposes. Accelerated depreciation up-fronts more of the cost, and therefore reduces the tax to be paid in early years – hence its attractiveness to management and the subsequent creation of a tax liability.

Debt is the most common form of liability. Each issuance is capitalised, and recognised on the balance sheet at original cost minus any principal repayments. The cost of debt – or interest – is then recognised through income statement. For example, if the outstanding debt balance were $1 million and the annualised interest rate 5%, the interest expense that year would be $50,000. Notably, interest payments are based on the balance sheet debt value multiplied by the effective interest rate on the debt, rather than on the timing of actual cash payments. This reduces the lumpiness that would otherwise arise if debt payments were only recognised in the period paid. However, it does mean that cash and accrual interest amounts can vary in any given period.

Typically, a company will have several debt issues outstanding, often with different structures and terms. While sometimes a company will seek to pay down its debt, frequently management will also intentionally retain a level of debt within the capital structure to enhance returns to equity. As a general rule, the more mature the business and the more tangible assets it has, the greater the gearing is likely to be. For example, a start-up online company will unlikely be able to secure much (if any) debt financing, whereas a water utility company with a long operating track record might well have more debt than equity on its balance sheet. It is therefore worth understanding management strategy with regards to capital structure, including whether it intends to roll over matured debt into new issuances or try to pay it down using cash.

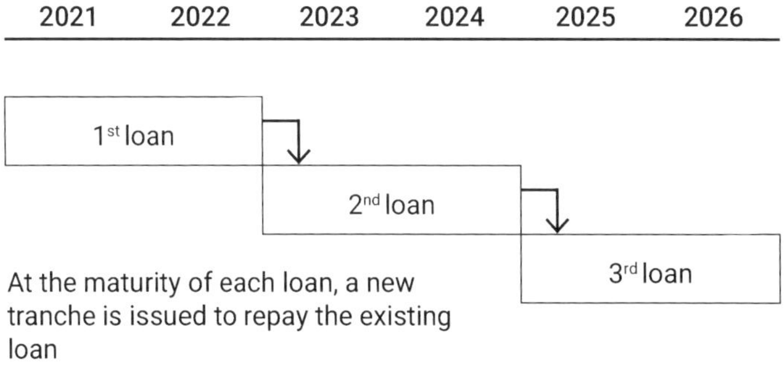

The final piece to our balance sheet equation is shareholder equity. This represents the residual value of assets after all liabilities have been accounted for – meaning, for example, that in the unlikely event a company had no liabilities, equity would be equal to assets. If financial statements were an entirely accurate representation of economic value, the book would end here and we would simply use the balance sheet equity value to dictate company value. Unfortunately though, that is very rarely the case, although book equity value is a helpful starting point for some business models where the majority of value is in tangible on-balance sheet assets.

Shareholder equity has several sub-categories, representing different sources of equity capital. Despite being the most relevant section of the balance sheet in terms of valuation, it is also normally the least analysed. The key and often most variable line item within shareholder equity is retained earnings – income statement net income minus dividends. If net income is positive and is not all being paid out in dividends, this item will increase over time, thereby increasing the value of shareholders' equity. Dividends will be touched on in detail later, but these are essentially payments to shareholders to provide a return in exchange for their investment (in a similar way that a lender would receive interest in return for lending).

The most substantial figure under shareholder equity will likely be contributed capital (also known as issued capital), as this is the amount contributed by the common shareholders. This might include capital from an initial public offering or secondary offering, for instance. It is sometimes broken out into two items: common stock (cash for common shares) and additional paid in capital (cash in excess of par value). The distinction for analytical purposes is of no real value, as par value is a relatively arbitrary number based on the lowest value that a company could sell shares for.

In the event that the company has a subsidiary – a company that it has majority but not full ownership of – as per the approach with the income statement, the financials are consolidated and a minority interest line is recognised. This minority interest line appears in the equity section and represents the pro-rata share of equity from the subsidiary that the company is not entitled to. In this instance, there will be a distinction in equity between 'equity' and 'equity attributable to shareholders in the company'. The former refers to equity including minority interests, while the latter is the more important figure for analytical purposes as it refers purely to shareholder equity value.

Other lines that some companies might have under equity include treasury stock and preferred stock. Treasury stock refers to shares in the company that have been repurchased but not cancelled. These shares have no voting rights and do not receive dividends. Companies typically acquire their own stock if they believe the share price materially understates the firm's fair value. Once shares have been repurchased, they can either be cancelled (in which case the per share value of income and equity rises) or kept on the balance sheet in treasury and cancelled or reissued at a later point. There are often mixed feelings from shareholders about this practice, as using company cash to trade in company shares can be a management distraction and is likely not leveraging on their area of expertise. In addition, as share-based remuneration packages are increasingly common, there is always the risk that a share repurchase programme is launched with the intention of manufacturing a higher price for management to sell shares at, rather than creating shareholder value. Preferred stock, such as debt or equity, is issued by the company to raise funds. It is considered a 'hybrid' instrument, as it is junior to debt but senior to equity in the event of a liquidation. There are a range of features that preferred stock might be issued with, and in some cases the structure can even mean that it is classified as a liability instead of equity. Generally, however, it is an equity item, has no voting rights and the holder is entitled to a fixed dividend which, while not assured, must be paid before any dividends to shareholders are distributed. Normally, preferred equity dividends are paid as a fixed percent of the preference share par value, although occasionally they are structured so that the holder participates in dividend growth when higher dividends are achievable.

Cash flow statement

The cash flow statement is the simplest and most intuitive of the financial statements. It details the actual cash transactions over the period under review – cash coming in, cash going out. No accounting wizardry is therefore required. As a result, relative to the income statement, it is far more of a blunt instrument to measure performance in any given year. However, it is also the most tangible measure of operational activity over time and is therefore equally (if not more) important than others.

The cash flow statement breaks down into operating activity, investment activity and financing activity – different from the revenue, costs and profit structure of the income statement. There is no 'net income' number at the bottom of the cash flow statement. Rather, the concluding line is simply a 'change in cash position' – a figure that sums operational, investing and financing flows all together. This change in cash position figure, when added to the prior-year balance sheet cash balance, equals the current-year cash figure.

Net income	
Depreciation	
Receivables	Adjustments to transform income statement operating income after tax into operating cash flow
Inventory	
Payables	
Income taxes payable	
Operating cash flow	Summed total

Capital expenditure	Cash generated or spent on investments
Acquisitions/divestments	
Investing cash flow	Summed total
Issuance of common stock	
Dividends (current year)	Cash flows from funding activity
Change in long-term debt	
Financing cash flow	Summed total
Net change in cash	Operating + investing + financing cash flow

Starting with cash flow from operations, this details the cash flows within the normal course of business. There are two means of calculating this: the direct and indirect method. The indirect method is used in the example above. Both sum to the same figure, but the process to arrive at that figure varies. The direct method is simplest, summing cash receipts against cash costs to equal cash flow from operations. The non-direct method however is more often used, as it can be easily calculated using the income statement and balance sheet data alone, with no further disclosure required. Adjustments to net income include adding back the period's non-cash charges, such as depreciation and amortisation, plus unwinding operational accrual items (receivables, inventory and payables) by taking the current- and prior-year balance sheet differences. So for example, if in 2020 a company's balance sheet receivables were \$1,000 and they rose to \$1,200 in 2021, we would determine that through the year of 2021 a net amount of \$200 had been recognised in the income statement for which cash had yet to be received. That \$200 would therefore need to be subtracted from net income for the purpose of calculating the actual cash generation over the period. For analytical purposes, the operating cash flow number should be compared with the firm's operating profit. If there is consistently a substantial difference between cash profits and accrual operating profits, it is worth exploring why.

Cash flow from investments details the amounts generated or spent on investments. Inflows can be from an acquisition, but are more often the result of capital expenditure within the company. When analysing this line, capital expenditure (CAPEX) is typically split between growth CAPEX (expenditure to increase service/production capability) and maintenance CAPEX (expenditure to maintain service/production levels, such as replacing old equipment, etc). This will not be broken out in the financial statement, but it is helpful if management can provide it, as it will give us some insight into what the long-term relationship between operating and investment cash flow will look like once it matures beyond the growth phase.

Inflows into cash flow from investments are typically smaller than outflows and less sustainable over time. An inflow might, for example, be generated by the sales of fixed assets (such as land, a building or equipment) or the sale of investment securities (any bonds/equity held by the company and sold). While for most companies these inflows are proportionally very small relative to operational cash flows, for some financial companies they can account for the majority of activity – the distinctions for which are covered in a later chapter.

Finally, cash flow from financing is the last section of the cash flow statement, detailing financing transactions with debtors and equity holders. An inflow would result from an issuance of debt and/or equity. An outflow would result from the payment of dividends to shareholders or the repayment of principal to debt holders. In the event that management buys shares to either cancel or keep in treasury, the cash used to make the share purchases will also appear in this section. It will be very roughly equivalent to the average share price during the share buyback period multiplied by the numbers of shares purchased.

As noted at the start, the cash flow statement does not sum to a net income figure. We can however calculate performance measures to assess it over time. The most commonly used are free cash flow to the firm, and free cash to equity. Free cash flow to the firm reflects cash flow to both debt and equity investors. It is calculated as cash flow from operations (CFO) plus the income statement interest expense adjusted for tax, minus capital expenditure (CAPEX).

$$\text{Cash flow to the firm} = \text{CFO} + \text{Int. exp.}\ (1 - \text{Tax rate}) - \text{CAPEX}$$

This measure is the key input when using intrinsic valuation to value a company and will come up again later. It offers a good balance between being a tangible measure of performance while not being overwhelmed by the volatility that funding activity can bring. Alternatively, if we desire to understand cash flow specifically to equity holders over time, the cash flow to equity is a more direct measure. This is calculated as cash flow from operations minus capital expenditure, plus/minus any debt repaid/issued.

$$\text{Cash flow to equity} = \text{CFO} - \text{CAPEX} +/- \text{Net debt issued}$$

As a benchmark of performance, this benefits from being specific to equity. However, it can be a highly volatile figure when there are large changes in net debt due to issuance/repayment. Like cash flow to the firm, this can be used as an input when using the intrinsic valuation method.

The final cash flow summary calculation that is normally made is a simple change in cash position. This is equal to cash flow from operations (CFO) plus cash flow from investment (CFI) plus cash flow from financing (CFF).

$$\text{Change in cash position} = \text{CFO} + \text{CFI} + \text{CFF}$$

While this figure may not be actively used in ratios, it is a figure that needs calculating if we want to build a financial model and determine what the end of period cash position is (prior-year cash plus change in cash position).

STANDARDISING FINANCIAL STATEMENT STATISTICS

Financial statements can certainly appear to offer an overwhelming mass of information. Therefore, to make analysis more digestible, we can manage this information using financial ratios. These standardise key relationships in the financial statements for comparative purposes. This allows the analyst to compare companies, no matter their size, the currency they report in or the sector in which they operate. This also makes it easier to identify, and therefore project, trends.

Ratios can be grouped into four categories: activity ratios, profitability ratios, liquidity ratios and debt ratios. These ratios should be compared to industry norms, as well as against the firm's own history. In the event that there is a material deviation, it will be worth scrutinising why that is. For example, is the deviation suggestive of a 'new norm' or is that ratio liable to mean-revert back to its historical or peer average? In any case, judgements should be made in the context of what differentiates the company from its competition and changing variables (technology, consumer preferences, etc). In addition, consider materiality – if it is a ratio which is not of material significance to the company, do not get overly concerned about finding the root cause of any difference. Not every ratio is of equal importance, and indeed, different companies will likely require a different prioritisation in terms of which ones are most important.

Activity ratios

Activity ratios are measures of how effectively a company is managing its balance sheet to generate revenue and cash. There are a variety of ways that this can be done, but the primary measures are asset turnover and working capital ratios.

Working capital refers to capital that supports the business in day-to-day operations – distinct from investment capital. What we want to assess is the length of time it takes to turn the firm's cash investment in inventory back into cash, in the form of collections from the sales of that inventory. The shorter the period required, the better. While the difference may be of limited impact for low-growth, stable businesses, if a company is expected to grow, it can create considerable cash pressure.

The key components of working capital are the balance sheet items of receivables, inventory and payables. If a company has a lot of capital tied up in receivables and inventory, this can be a considerable drain on resources and limit growth. Payables meanwhile are a liability on the balance sheet, and delaying payment to suppliers relieves some of the working capital pressure businesses endure. This is reflected in the below calculation.

$$\text{Working capital} = \text{Receivables} + \text{Inventory} - \text{Payables}$$

Absolute figures are however of limited help when seeking to compare across time or company. We therefore transform this data into days outstanding – a measure that gives us insight into the time practicalities of working capital arrangements.

$$\text{Receivable days} = \frac{\text{Balance sheet: receivables}}{\text{Income statement: cost of goods}} \times 365$$

$$\text{Inventory days} = \frac{\text{Balance sheet: inventory}}{\text{Income statement: cost of goods}} \times 365$$

$$\text{Payable days} = \frac{\text{Balance sheet: payables}}{\text{Income statement: cost of goods}} \times 365$$

For receivable days, typically you would expect only a couple of days at most for food retail businesses, whereas for a manufacturer they might extend to 30–90 days. As a general rule, companies serving individuals will have fewer receivable days, whereas companies serving other companies (typically lower down in the value chain of a product or service) will have more. If a company has a materially greater number of receivable days than its peers, you should question if extended payment terms are being used to gain a competitive advantage. If so, this does not provide a very sustainable edge over peers and will likely expose the company to risk of non-payment during periods of financial or economic stress.

Inventory days also vary greatly between businesses. A high-end gallery may well have months of inventory, whereas any retail outlet selling fresh produce, such as a butcher, would likely only have a week or so. As a very general rule, the higher value the product and the more it holds its value, the greater the likelihood of longer inventory days. All else equal, shorter and stable inventory days typically suggest that a company's processes and order management systems are likely better than their peers', allowing them to better anticipate demand. Beyond the cash flow benefits, having shorter inventory days also means that a company can reduce sell-through risks that might otherwise arise from seasonality and changes in technology and fashion. While a rise in inventory days may suggest that a company is at risk of writing down inventory due to an inability to clear stock, it could also be a positive indicator of high expected sales, for example due to a new product launch. So keep an open mind.

Payables and receivables are different sides of the same coin. A receivable recognised in one company's balance sheet will create payables of equal value in those of its customers. The greater the number of payable days, the better. In some cases, companies have even been able to achieve negative working capital days by having longer payable days than inventory and receivables collectively, although this is rare. Smaller high-growth companies in particular benefit from having extended payables, as this reduces the working capital funding required to expand the business.

Working capital days can be summarised by adding inventory days and receivables days, then subtracting payable days. This equals how long cash is tied up in the whole selling process, which can often be months.

The other measure of activity – total asset turnover – is a gauge of how effectively the company uses assets to create revenue. The higher the ratio, the more effectively the firm is 'sweating' its balance sheet assets.

$$\text{Total asset turnover} = \frac{\text{Revenue}}{\text{Average of total assets}}$$

While a high ratio is normally encouraging, if it is abnormally high relative to peers, this should be explored. Maybe it's the case that the company is efficient, but it might also indicate that the company is running near capacity and requires further investment. Bear in mind also that this is not just a measure of operational efficiency, but also of capital efficiency. For example, a lower asset turnover relative to peers could be a consequence of poor operating metrics, but equally might be due to a higher portion of its balance sheet lying idle in cash.

Liquidity ratios

Liquidity ratios are employed by analysts to determine the firm's ability to pay its short term liabilities. For most companies, and across most periods, these measures will not be highly relevant. However, during periods of economic stress and for companies that are at risk of default, they are worth calculating. While liquidity risk is often assessed alongside leverage, the two measures are distinct. For example, you may own your house with only a modest mortgage, but could still struggle to meet near-term mortgage payments if you do not have enough liquid assets.

The current ratio is the best-known measure of liquidity, and the easiest to calculate.

$$\text{Current ratio} = \frac{\text{Current assets}}{\text{Current liabilities}}$$

The higher the ratio, the more likely it is that the company will be able to pay its short-term bills. Anything near or below one suggests that the company is potentially unable to cover near-term obligations with current assets. As with all the ratios though, further scrutiny should be applied before jumping to conclusions, as factors like seasonality can often skew figures in a given period.

If you want to take a more forensic approach to liquidity analysis, the quick ratio is a more conservative measure of a company's financial position. Rather than placing current assets as the numerator, cash, marketable securities and receivables are summed – the key difference being that inventory is excluded. This is more complex to calculate, but in practice is often a more relevant measure, as if the company is having difficulty selling inventory, this is not a current asset that can be counted on to convert and meet liabilities in the short term.

$$\text{Quick ratio} = \frac{\text{Cash + Marketable securities + Receivables}}{\text{Current liabilities}}$$

Financial leverage ratios

Financial leverage ratios measure a firm's financial leverage and ability to meet its overall obligations. As with liquidity ratios, there are multiple ways this can be assessed. The three key measures typically used are leverage, net debt to equity, net debt to EBITDA, and interest cover.

Assets to equity is the broadest definition of leverage and includes all outstanding equity and liabilities. This is of particular use when assessing financial firms – businesses where non-debt obligations, such as deposits, can make up a considerable part of total liabilities. It is calculated by dividing assets by equity.

$$\text{Leverage} = \frac{\text{Assets}}{\text{Equity}}$$

The greater the leverage, the higher the risk – but also the greater the equity upside when things go well. As we will find out when assessing profitability ratios, this will be a key input that influences the overall return to equity. This figure can vary widely between companies in different industries. For instance, banks frequently have over 10x assets to equity, whereas industrial firms typically have below 4x. We can also convert the ratio to establish what proportion of balance sheet funding is equity by dividing one by the ratio. For example, if the company has an assets to equity ratio of 5x, that is equivalent to saying that 20% (1 ÷ 5 = 0.2) of balance sheet funding is in equity.

While the assets to equity ratio is helpful as a measure of obligations to equity, to specifically measure a company's capital structure with regards to debt versus equity, the net debt to equity ratio is more practical. To calculate, include all balance sheet debt minus cash in the numerator, and total equity in the denominator.

$$\text{Net debt to equity ratio} = \frac{\text{Net debt}}{\text{Total equity}}$$

Increases and decreases in this ratio suggest a greater or lesser reliance on debt as a source of financing. Across most industries, it is the most commonly referenced leverage ratio used in discussions regarding a company's target capital structure. Sometimes however, a company will frame it in terms of 'debt to equity', and not subtract cash from debt in order to simplify the relationship.

Finally, interest coverage. This is an income statement-derived ratio and reflects how comfortably the company can pay interest from earnings before interest and tax.

$$\text{Interest coverage ratio} = \frac{\text{Earnings before interest and tax}}{\text{Interest payments}}$$

The lower this ratio, the more likely it is that the firm will have difficulty meeting its debt payments. All else being equal, a higher ratio in this instance is preferable. If the coverage ratio is below one, that means interest payments are greater than earnings before interest and tax, and that is of course a considerable risk if the situation does not change. However, that does not necessarily mean that the firm is insolvent. Remember, income statement interest is based on capitalised debt multiplied by the interest rate, and not on actual cash payments. For example, if interest is only due at the time that the debt outstanding matures, and that debt payment can be covered by the issuance of more debt, then no interim cash payments will be required and the company can operate with an interest cover below one. This type of financing arrangement would however be risky, and would quickly unravel in the event that banks refused to lend more money when an existing issue became due.

Profitability ratios

Profitability ratios measure the overall performance of the firm. These are different to other measures that concentrate on single components of a company's financial or operational position/performance. While these measures therefore lack depth, the breadth of factors that they incorporate means that they are the single easiest way to summarise a company's return profile. When dealing with ratios that combine the balance sheet with an income statement item, averages of the period assessed and the prior period must be used for the balance sheet. This is to ensure that income is fairly compared to average equity or assets over the period, rather than simply a year-end snapshot. In addition, if quarterly or semi-annual income statement figures are being used, these will require annualising to make them applicable for any ratio – multiply by four in the case of quarterly numbers, and by two for semi-annual ones.

The most frequently used measure is the return on equity (ROE). This is calculated by dividing a company's net income by its average balance sheet equity. The percentage figure output is the annualised balance sheet equity growth rate, assuming no dividends are paid. The higher the ROE, the more 'profitable' the firm is considered to be.

$$\text{Return on equity} = \left(\frac{\text{Net income}}{\text{Average equity}}\right)$$

For instance, if a firm had balance sheet equity of $95 million in 2020 and $105 million in 2021, plus made a profit of $10 million in 2021, its return on equity would be 10% ($10 million ÷ $100 million).

If we want to explore what is driving a changing level in a company's ROE, we need to break it out into its key component parts – namely, net profit margin, asset turnover and leverage ratio. These three components, when summed together, equal the ROE, and therefore can be broken down to isolate which factor is varying. Normally, it is the case that net margin will be the most variable, followed by asset turnover, then leverage.

$$\text{Return on equity} = \left(\begin{array}{c}\text{Net profit}\\ \text{margin}\end{array}\right) \times \left(\begin{array}{c}\text{Asset}\\ \text{turnover}\end{array}\right) \times \left(\begin{array}{c}\text{Leverage}\\ \text{ratio}\end{array}\right)$$

$$\text{Return on equity} = \left(\frac{\text{Net income}}{\text{Sales}}\right) \times \left(\frac{\text{Sales}}{\text{Assets}}\right) \times \left(\frac{\text{Assets}}{\text{Equity}}\right)$$

The relationship between margin, turnover and leverage will vary largely, based on the type of business it is calculated for. For instance, a supermarket may well have a high asset turnover but only make a low margin, while a bank may have a low margin but a high leverage ratio.

If we want to assess only the operational profitability of a company, and therefore exclude leverage, the return on assets is a helpful adjusted version of the ROE ratio to achieve this. It multiplies only net profit margin by asset turnover and can be summarised by simply dividing the net income by average assets.

$$\text{Return on assets} = \frac{\text{Net income}}{\text{Average assets}}$$

$$\text{Return on assets} = \left(\frac{\text{Net income}}{\text{Sales}}\right) \times \left(\frac{\text{Sales}}{\text{Assets}}\right)$$

Using this measure, it matters not if a company has excessive leverage or a conservative debt position. Both will be treated almost equally under this measure. I say 'almost' because interest expense is still accounted for in net income. This measure is particularly helpful when assessing industrial companies, utilities or banks – businesses that have the majority of their value in tangible assets and whose leverage can vary significantly.

The shareholder's return: dividends

Beyond an analysis of financial statements, a further aspect of financial analysis is the assessment of the company's dividend history, if any. Dividends are theoretically the single most important line item for an investment valuation. Many companies do not pay them, but regardless of a company's growth prospects or size, other than having its shares acquired in an acquisition or merger, without dividends the company's effective value is zero. It is that simple.

Shares in a company are not a currency simply to be traded. They only have value as there is an expectation that in exchange for an investment there will be a return. Of course, many companies do not pay a dividend in the early years, as there may well be better investment opportunities that allow them to grow earnings and produce a greater dividend further down the road – thereby creating greater shareholder value. However, be in no doubt that even Amazon or Facebook will someday mature and make payments to shareholders. Otherwise, if no distribution to shareholders was ever expected in the future, why would their shares be worth anything?

For the company, dividends represent a transfer of assets (cash) from it to shareholders. When a shareholder becomes entitled to a dividend, the share price should drop by the amount that shareholders are entitled to receive. For instance, if a firm traded at $20 and announced a $2 dividend, then come the 'ex-dividend date', its share price should drop to $18 ($20 – $2 = $18). This is important to understand and goes to show that looking at the share price chart of a company can often only tell part of the story when it comes to actual total shareholder returns.

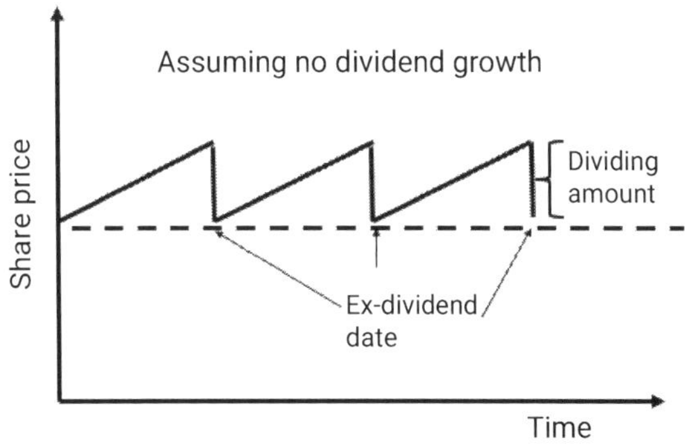

In terms of the actual process for a dividend distribution, this starts with an announcement from the board regarding the amount paid (note that this is not a management decision). The next stage is the ex-dividend date, which is the cut-off date for when shareholders are entitled to the dividend. After the ex-dividend date, new shareholders will not receive the announced dividend. The final date is the dividend distribution date – which is when the dividend is actually paid. The difference between these stages can be weeks, and even months.

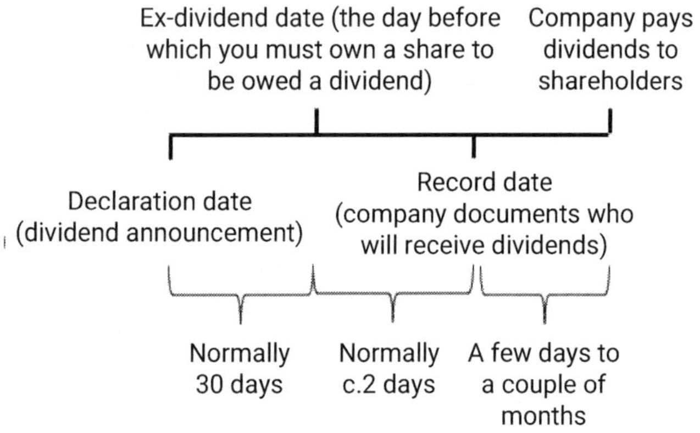

Dividends come in three forms: regular, special and liquidating. When a company pays a dividend on a consistent basis, this is called a 'regular' dividend. Payments could be quarterly, semi-annually or annually. Management often aims to pay out a particular portion of profits. This is known as the dividend payout ratio and is calculated as dividends divided by earnings.

$$\text{Dividend payout ratio} = \frac{\text{Dividend}}{\text{Earnings}}$$

Sometimes, an absolute dividend amount is targeted – common in markets such as the US. However, while this provides shareholders with greater income outlook certainty, it lacks the flexibility of a ratio, and therefore can create significant disappointment if earnings are weak and the dividend amount cannot be paid.

Dividends termed as 'special' are irregular dividends. They are one-off special payments which are often made in addition to regular dividends when conditions are particularly favourable, such as when operations have been particularly strong or there is excessive cash idle on the balance sheet. Liquidating dividends are the least frequent. These occur when a company goes out of business and distributes the proceeds to shareholders. For tax purposes, a liquidating dividend is treated as a return of capital.

Some companies also pay stock dividends. No cash is received by the shareholder. Instead, each shareholder just receives new additional shares in proportion to their holding. For the company, this is a means of paying a 'dividend' while not having to reduce the firm's cash balance. Many shareholders however frown upon this form of dividend, seeing it as little more than financial gimmickry.

Beyond dividends, the board can also decide to use company cash to realise shareholder value by other means – namely, share repurchase. This is a transaction in which a company buys back shares of its own common stock either in the market or by direct negotiation with shareholders. It is typically done when the board believes that the company is significantly undervalued. The shares purchased can then either be held on the firm's balance sheet and sold when the price rises, used as part of management remuneration, or cancelled. If the shares are held on the balance sheet or given to management, then there is no change in the number of outstanding shares. However, if they are cancelled, that means that the outstanding number of shares is reduced and therefore per share measures – such as earnings per share – increase. Share buybacks that actually cancel shares are generally far more favoured by investors. Indeed for individual investors, the purchase and cancellation of shares often represent a more tax efficient form of return than dividends, as for many their capital gains tax rate is lower than their income tax rate.

Summary

Financial statements offer a window into a company's financial health and performance. There are three separate statements: the balance sheet, the income statement and the cash flow statement. The balance sheet is an account of what is owned and owed and who owns company shares. The income statement is a performance report matching sales and costs. The cash flow statement is a report of company cash flows. These statements are a mass of numbers, but by transforming them into ratios that can be compared across time and company, they can fortunately be made easily digestible. The key ratios cover activity, liquidity, leverage, profitability and dividends.

Fact Finding

Fortunately for investors, company disclosure does not end at the financial statements. An annual report to shareholders must be published and an annual general meeting held. While some companies treat these as an empty formality, often they are a rich source of information, providing context and insight that will help shape well-informed conclusions.

The annual report

A company's annual report is a report to shareholders that details the company's finances and activities over the year. It can often run to hundreds of pages, although key conclusions can normally be drawn out in 20 to 40 minutes for those who know their way around these documents.

The key components to a company's financial report can vary. Typically however, it will start with financial highlights, there will be a letter to shareholders from the chairman and/or CEO, as well as a management discussion section, the financial statements, the auditor's report, and finally the footnotes to the financial statements. These reports are often accompanied with colourful photos, charts and graphs to emphasise key points that management wants to draw the reader's attention to.

The most important section of the report, and a priority for any financial analysis, will be the financial statements – analysis of which was covered in the last chapter. These statements are supplemented by the footnotes to the financial statements, used to explain key assumptions in the financial statements and accounting policies adopted by the company. Commonly, this includes further details on the depreciation policy, valuation of inventory and treatment of intangibles. Also within the footnotes, segment reporting can be found. In the US, for example, public companies are required to break out details for any segment that accounts for more than 10% of revenue, profit or assets. For more complex companies operating with multiple product lines or service offerings, this breakdown is a very helpful insight into what is really driving underlying performance and how that is changing over time.

Beyond helpful financial statement insights, the footnotes also include details on related party transactions. These are defined by a company doing business with a person or organisation where there is an existing relationship. They are uncommon, and if present can present scope for a serious conflict of interest. Therefore, an assessment should be made to understand the rationale for any such transaction and whether it in any way disadvantages shareholders. The footnotes also sometimes contain an explanatory paragraph when a material loss is probable but the amount cannot be reasonably estimated. These "uncertainties" may be down to the valuation or realisation of asset values, or to litigation – for example, if a company is being sued for a substantial amount in the context of its operations but it is not known whether it will be found guilty. This type of disclosure may be a signal of serious problems and would therefore require additional examination.

Beyond accounting details, the management discussion and analysis (MD&A) section is also an important source of information, providing context to the statements and insight into the company's strategy and goals. Public companies' management teams have to be very careful when communicating with those outside the company with regards to forward-looking statements, so the MD&A is a useful means of fairly disseminating information to all interested parties. Remember however that the MD&A section is a tool for management teams to communicate directly with shareholders, so they will likely weave a narrative that suits their purpose. This might include emphasising positives, underplaying risks, attempting to absolve themselves of responsibility when performance is weak, and attributing success to their own initiatives.

Of less importance, although still relevant, are the details of the auditor's report. This section of the annual report can be quite wordy, and therefore typically an analyst will skip straight to the concluding opinion. An unqualified opinion (also known as a clean opinion) indicates that the auditor believes the statements are free from material omissions and errors. A qualified opinion is issued if the statements make any exceptions to the accounting principles, and an explanation of these exceptions is then detailed. Finally, an adverse opinion is issued by the auditor if the statements are not presented fairly or are materially nonconforming with accounting standards. Suffice to say, anything outside of a qualified opinion is extremely rare, and should raise some serious red flags when assessing a company.

The most renowned auditors globally are Deloitte, PwC, Ernst & Young (EY) and KPMG. For public companies, shareholders typically prefer the company use a large auditor with a good reputation, and for this reason, large public company audits are largely dominated by the 'top four'. Importantly, management does not choose the company's auditor – that would run the risk that it seeks out a friendly face to sign off on the reports. In theory, the shareholders should appoint the auditors, but in practice it is the shareholder representatives – the board or the audit committee of the board – that has the authority to hire the auditor. Despite this, history is littered with examples of companies that have been in cahoots with their auditor and misled investors for years. Think Enron, for example. While it's highly unlikely that you will stumble across a company that has been intentionally misleading investors, if you do not understand the business and why it generates the profits it does, it is best to stay away.

The annual general meeting

After the annual report is published, the company will hold an annual general meeting. This is a requirement for most companies, whether private or publicly listed, and any shareholder (no matter how small their position size) has a legal right to attend. The AGM is typically the only opportunity that investors have to engage with a company's management and board, and it is held not just to provide transparency but also so that interested parties can have a say on company decisions. In recent years, a particularly sensitive area that has aggravated shareholders has been senior management remuneration, and frustrated shareholders have often used the AGM as a forum to air their grievances. At the AGM, shareholders are also given the opportunity to vote on items such as the minutes of the previous year's AGM, election of board members, approval of the financial statements and ratification of director actions (such as a dividend payment).

A shareholder does not have to vote, but voting offers the most direct means for expressing any views or disagreements. In the instance that a shareholder cannot attend, a vote can still be made by proxy – either online or by mail. Many of the larger institutional asset managers investing in publicly listed companies now outsource voting to third parties known as proxy advisors or vote service providers. These are specialist companies that have the resources, experience and software to make reasonably informed voting choices on behalf of shareholders. Current providers include Institutional Shareholder Services (ISS) and Egan-Jones Ratings Company. While these companies offer a helpful steer, they are however often quite mechanical in how they vote and therefore can miss out on the nuance and insight that would otherwise come from a fundamental understanding of the company.

The nature of an AGM can range from a simple meeting to run through legal, administrative and voting matters to grand affairs with talks, food and entertainment. The best-known AGM is that held by Berkshire Hathaway, Warren Buffett's company. This has become known as a 'Woodstock for Capitalists', attracting over 10,000 attendees and including detailed speeches with regards to vision and outlook.

If AGM attendance is inconvenient or the company treats it as nothing more than a formality, there are also the post-results conference calls/webcasts often held by management of public companies (private companies far less so). These meetings can be attended by anyone, shareholder or not. They typically include a presentation (found on the company's website) and normally last for around an hour, with half the time dedicated to a management update and the other half to participant questions. Even if a call/webcast is not being held in the immediate future, the Investor Relations section of a company's website now often provides investors with a link to listen to historic calls and presentations. Quarterlies and press releases are of course also further sources of insight into a company's activity, albeit typically offering far less detail than a full annual report.

In addition to the AGM, companies can also call an EGM – an extraordinary general meeting. These shareholder meetings are scheduled outside of the AGM and are typically used to deal with urgent matters such as removing an executive or a legal matter. They are rare but, if called, shareholders should be made aware of location, date and the resolutions well in advance to provide adequate time for any preparation and/or research required. In terms of attendance, at least five members must be present for a public company's EGM, unless bylaws state otherwise. In the case of private companies, minimum attendance is two.

Summary

A company's report to shareholders can provide very helpful context for its financial statements, and often provides information that might help when forecasting forward. Bear in mind, however, that sections offering management commentary can sometimes be biased to serve senior management interests. A good analyst will however be able to differentiate fluff from fact, and objectively extract details that will help when forecasting.

PROJECT

Projecting returns

'If past history was all that is needed to play the game of money, the richest people would be librarians' – Warren Buffett

Facts, figures, thoughts and theories about a company are all very well, but these need to be shaped into a single value – the company value. There are two key components that need to be quantified to produce this: the return outlook and a discount rate (to account for risk and opportunity cost).

This chapter focuses on the return outlook, building on prior chapters to develop a thorough, quantitative, easily adaptable numerical forecast for future returns that can then be readily applied to a company's value.

However, for those seeking to make quick valuation decisions based on rough judgements, flick forward to the next chapter now. There is no shame in doing so, and indeed, many institutional investors intentionally prioritise covering many companies over conducting comprehensive analysis of single names. This is especially true for those performing a relative valuation. Broad generalisation can be made about headline figures, such as what free cash flow or net income growth may be over the near and long term. For instance, a simple 'I expect profits to grow 5% annually over the next three years and decelerate to 3% thereafter' allows for quick decision-making and can be a practical form of projection for mature companies with stable performance. Companies are however complex, with multiple moving variables driving end outcomes, especially for growth companies. To adequately incorporate such detail to make a thorough determination of future direction, a full financial model should be the preferred.

All you need to create a financial model is a computer with Microsoft Excel installed and some common sense, time and patience. The end outcome should be a comprehensive and easily adjustable set of forward-looking financial statements based on inputted assumptions. The ability to create such a model is a very powerful skillset and, beyond company valuation, it will be helpful for activities including company strategy development, budgeting forecasts and M&A, to name a few. Whether you work in investment banking, in equity research, at an accounting firm, in a firm's corporate development/ finance department or at an asset management firm, the steps learnt in this chapter will likely be of particular relevance.

From the outset, however, be mindful that these are estimates you will be creating, and therefore the assumptions will almost certainly require updating with the passing of time. The beauty of a financial model is that it is live. Once completed, future adjustments are easy to make. We should therefore be ready to adapt and change our expectations as new information comes to light. As the famous writer and lecturer Dale Carnegie said, 'If you are wrong, admit it quickly and emphatically.'

The process

Financial modelling is methodical. And while it may seem complex at first, it should quickly become intuitive. Its key components include assumptions, supporting schedules and, finally, the financial statements themselves. While the output might look like a mass of numbers, the only actual area that numbers will be inputted (hard coded) will be the assumptions section. The rest of the model will be formula driven, and automatically update as assumptions adjust.

In terms of process, there are four key stages to the development of a financial model:

1. Input and format historical data
2. Detail assumptions
3. Set up supporting schedules
4. Link up the financial statements

While following all four steps may be time-consuming and laborious at first, with experience the time required should decline, especially if you can get your head around Excel shortcuts.

1. Prepare

First, input the company's historical financial statement data. If the company is publicly listed, this should be available on its website within the section marked 'Investor Relations'. The longer the period covered, the more identifiable key trends will become and the further insight you will have into the company's sensitivities (policy, business cycle, etc). Inputting numbers is however a relatively dull and time-consuming task, so in most cases analysts limit themselves to inputting three years of historical performance.

With regards to formatting, it is recommended that you keep all of your financial model on one Excel tab, for the simple reason that it is easier to navigate and make links between the statements. Structure the worksheet so that, in order of vertical descent, assumptions come first, followed by the income statement, balance sheet, cash flow statement and, finally, the supporting schedules. To make the document clear, freeze the date row so that no matter how far down you are in the document, the period date is visible. In addition, remove the Excel gridlines to smarten the spreadsheet up and format cells so that historic and projected numbers are colour coded differently and therefore easy to differentiate. The typical standard used is blue for hard coded figures (ones manually inputted) and black for all the formulas.

Once we have inputted historical data and dealt with formatting, modifications are needed to simplify or add further detail where necessary. Simplification is required as financial statements often have an overwhelming level of detail, and similar line items can be combined without any material loss of output accuracy. For example, companies sometimes break out their 'payables' into several different lines, when in practice these lines are very similar in nature and could be merged together. Doing this early on will save time later and make the model easier to navigate for the future.

In some cases, greater detail is advantageous, and the footnotes to the financial statements can be used to flesh out certain line items. This might be the case, for example, when dealing with operating expenses, and items such as selling expenses can be further broken down (for instance between commission and advertising). This is helpful when a line item is material in the context of the financial statement and its component parts are dissimilar.

2. Develop assumptions (A)

Developing assumptions is the most critical step in terms of our own input. It takes all our insights from the assessment phase and quantifies that into assumptions that will drive the model. First however, the historic assumptions need to be reverse engineered, so that historic performance, positions and trends are known. This requires calculating for items such as revenue growth, margins, balance sheet relationships and the dividend payout, as per the below example template. In the template, many of the assumptions are shown as a percentage of sales. This simply means dividing the item by the company's sales figure. For example, to calculate the historic distribution expense assumption, first input the equal sign, then divide the distribution expense figure by sales (= distribution expense/sales). Once historic calculations are completed, the forward-looking assumptions can then be hard coded in. It is these that will drive the forecasts.

Income statement	
Sales growth	YoY % growth
Gross margin	Gross profit ÷ Sales
Distribution expense	YoY % growth or as a % of Sales
Marketing & admin expense	YoY % growth or as a % of Sales
Research expense	YoY % growth or as a % of Sales
Depreciation	% of Sales
Long-term debt interest expense	% of Total long-term average debt
Tax Rate	% of EBIT

Balance sheet	
Capital asset turnover ratio	Sales as a % of Average PPE
Receivable days (sales basis)	(Receivables ÷ Sales) × 365
Inventory days (COGS basis)	(Inventory ÷ Costs) × 365
Payable days (COGS basis)	(Payables ÷ Costs) × 365
Income tax payable	(% of Tax expense)
Long-term debt	Local currency amount outstanding
Common share capital	Local currency amount outstanding
Dividend payout ratio	% of Profit

Note that the operating expense items can be calculated as either a percentage of sales or as a year-on-year (YoY) percentage growth figure. Your choice of calculation should be based on the extent to which the operating expense in question is correlated with sales performance (normally visible from past performance). For example, it may well be the case that higher marketing expenditure will drive higher sales, and therefore calculating as a percent of sales is preferable. Conversely, research and development may change more independently, and therefore an independent growth calculation should be developed. As a very broad generalisation, for more mature companies it is advisable to use an independent year-on-year growth figure, as there will likely be greater operating leverage, while for growth companies, a percentage of sales assumption is likely to be more representative of spending and sales patterns.

Very importantly, not every assumption will require equal effort to project. Most balance sheet assumptions, for example, should be stable and largely based off long-term averages or trends. And indeed, debt and equity are normally kept flat unless you have a particular view otherwise. Meanwhile, sales growth can swing widely from year-to-year and, although to a far lesser extent, gross margin and operating expenses can vary also. Ultimately, for the moment, do not concern yourself with fine-tuning assumptions, as the output from the financial statements may well prompt you to make further amendments. For example, if the outcome of the forecast is that debt ratios will rise beyond a safe level, you will likely want to go back and adjust either your equity issuance assumption or reduce growth expectations to reflect capital structure constraints.

1. Supporting schedules (ss)

The next step is to develop supporting schedules. These are used so that we do not have to input complex formulas into a single cell come developing the financial statements. The key ones include the company's debt schedule, PP&E (property, plant and equipment) schedule and retained earnings schedule. You will note that for the moment these will only be set up, as, with the exception of the debt schedule, they can only be completed with the development of the income statement.

Depreciation schedule

Beginning of period	Prior period net PP&E
CAPEX/Additions (disposals)	End period net PP&E + Depreciation expense – Beginning PPE
Depreciation Expense	Sales × Depreciation expense (a)
End period net PP&E	Sales ÷ Capital asset turnover (a)

Retained earnings schedule

Beginning of Period	Prior-year retained earnings
Net income	Net income
Dividends	Net income × Dividend (a)
RE end of period	Prior-year retained earnings + Net income – Dividends

Interest schedule

Beginning of period	Prior-year ending period
Additions (repayments)	Current year LT debt (a) – Prior-year LT debt (a)
LTD end of period	Prior year + Additions (repayments)
Long-term debt interest	Prior/current LT debt average × Interest (a)

(a) = assumption

LT = long term

The output from the depreciation schedule will be used in the balance sheet (end of period PPE) and cash flow statement (depreciation and CAPEX). The output from retained earnings schedule will be used for the balance sheet (end of period retained earnings). And finally, the output debt from the debt schedule will be used in both the balance sheet (end of period debt) and income statement (interest expense). Note that in each instance, these schedules start with a historic figure – the beginning period (equal to the prior period end).

For instance, if the retained earnings for 2021 are to be projected, the beginning debt balance would be equal to the prior-year figure. While the calculation for PPE and retained earnings is standard, there are different layers of complexity for long-term debt. It can, for instance, be broken out into different debt issues and the interest expense calculated separately for each one. This is often relevant if the company is making significant changes to its capital structure or is in financial distress. Flick forward to the leverage buyout chapter if you want a more detailed debt schedule for your model (although this is unnecessary in most cases).

1. Develop the income statement

Next, we move to the income statement and start using formulas to create an automated financial statement. First, forecast down to the EBIT line using sales and margin assumptions. Then, use the interest expense output from the supporting schedule for the interest line, solve for tax and sum for net income.

Revenues	YoY % growth (a)
Cost of goods sold	Revenue - Gross profit
Gross profit	Revenue × Gross margin
Distribution expenses	YoY or as a % of Sales
Marketing and administration	YoY or as a % of Sales
Research and development	YoY or as a % of Sales
EBIT (operating profit)	Gross profit - Operating expenses
Interest	Interest expense (ss)
Income before taxes	EBIT - Interest
Taxes	EBIT × (1 - Tax rate (a))
Net income	Income before taxes - Taxes

(a)= assumptions
(ss)= supporting schedule

In instances where there is a year-on-year growth assumption, the formula used should be equal to the prior-year cell multiplied by one plus the percentage growth assumption. For example, if sales had been $100 and you expected 15% growth this year, the calculation for the sales cell would be $100 × (1 + 15%) = $115. In the event that percentage of sales is used, the cell is multiplied by the percentage of sales assumption. So, if sales were projected to be $115 and the distribution expense was calculated as 15%, the calculation for the distribution expense cell for that period would be $115 × 15% = $17.5.

2. Start on the balance sheet

The balance sheet is the next financial statement to develop. How complex this part is will be based on the level of company disclosure and simplifications made. Again, as with the income statement, treat this methodically. Outside of forward assumptions, financial statement modelling is a science, not an art.

The key components of assets are cash, inventory, receivables and PP&E (property, plant and equipment). To calculate the cash projection, the formula is equal to the prior-year closing cash balance plus the current-year net cash change. The net cash change is an output of the cash flow statement, and therefore this requires the completion of the cash flow statement to finalise. For receivables, sales are divided by 365 to determine the per day sales figure, and this is then inflated by the receivable days assumption to equal the balance sheet receivables figure. Likewise with inventory, but instead of sales as the numerator, cost is used. For PP&E, the value should be equal to the ending balance calculated in the support schedule for that year.

For liabilities, payables are calculated using the same methodology as inventory, but with payables as the balance sheet input. Deferred taxes are calculated by multiplying income statement tax by the deferred tax assumption, and the debt line is a direct feed into the debt assumption. For equity, common stock and additional stock link directly to their respective assumptions and retained earnings are derived from the supporting schedule.

Cash	Add net change in cash (CF statement)
Receivables	(Sales ÷ 365) × Receivable days (a)
Inventory	(Costs ÷ 365) × Receivable days (a)
PP&E	End of period PP&E (ss)
Assets	Sum all asset lines
Payables	(Costs ÷ 365) × Receivable days (a)
Income taxes payable	Tax expense × Income tax payable (a)
Long-term debt	Long-term debt (a)
Liabilities	Sum all liabilities lines
Common stock	Common stock (a)
Additional paid in capital	Paid in capital (a)
Retained earnings	Prior period + Retained earnings (ss)
Equity	Sum all equity lines

(a)= assumptions
(ss)= supporting schedule

Remember, there are no negative balances on the balance sheet, only positive. For instance, if cash turns negative due to cash outflows, the required response is to adjust assumptions to reflect that the company in this situation would either reduce growth to manage working capital, issue debt or equity, or sell assets such as 'investments' in order to maintain a positive balance.

3. Cash flow statement

The cash flow statement is the final stage. Like the other two statements, it is entirely formula driven and automated to adjust as assumptions become updated. There is a simple principle when forecasting for the cash flow statement. Outside of retained earnings and cash, if there is a year-on-year change in a balance sheet item, this must be reflected in the cash flow statement. It is therefore noticeable that most of the equations used for the cash flow lines are based on simply the current period minus the prior period. Note that in the case of assets, a rise between periods means an outflow or deferred benefit, and therefore a negative sign is required at the start of the formula. For liabilities or equity, a rise between periods equals an inflow or deferred cost, and therefore it is positive. If you encounter a more complex balance sheet than the one in the example, ensure that this approach is applied consistently to all assets/liabilities, otherwise the net change in cash will not equal the change in all other balance sheet items.

Starting with operating cash flow, the first line input is the income statement net income. The following lines then unwind the accruals used in the income statement – deferred items and non-cash charges such as depreciation. The add-back of depreciation should be equal to the depreciation output calculated in the PP&E. For the deferred items (payables, inventory and receivables), simply subtract the prior-period balance sheet amount from the current period. In the case of receivables and inventory, as these are asset amounts, a minus will be required at the beginning of the formula to reflect that any increase is a cash flow subtraction. As an illustration, if balance sheet receivables rose from $100 in 2021 to $150 in 2022, this would mean that an extra $50 of non-cash revenue had been recognised over the year, which would therefore need subtracting when calculating for the cash figure. For payables, no such minus sign is needed, as it is a liability line, and a rise in payables means payment has been delayed, and therefore the cash outflow is yet to occur.

For the investment cash flows, capital expenditure is likely to be the key (if not only) line for most company forecasts. It is equal to the calculated output in the supporting schedule. The key difficulty will arise when dealing with a banking model, when investment flows become more complex. For this reason, the steps required to develop a bank model and valuation are dealt with separately later in the book.

Finally, for financing activities, any change in debt or equity amounts is recognised by subtracting the current-year amount by the prior-year amount on the balance sheet. For example, if balance sheet common equity had risen from $140 million to $160 million between 2020 and 2021, that would suggest a $20 million cash inflow had occurred during the year. The 'dividends' cash flow is equal to the dividend assumptions within the supporting schedule for that period – net profit multiplied by the payout assumption.

Net income	Input from income statement
Depreciation	Input from (ss)
Receivables	-(Current period - Prior period)
Inventory	-(Current period - Prior period)
Payables	Current period - Prior period
Income taxes payable	Current period - Prior period
Operating cash flow	Summed total
Capital expenditure	CAPEX (ss)
Investing cash flow	Summed total
Issuance of common stock	Current period - Prior period
Dividends (current year)	-(Dividends (ss))
Change in long-term debt	Current period - Prior period
Financing cash flow	Summed total
Net change in cash	Operating CF + Investing CF + Financing CF

(a)= assumptions
(ss)= supporting schedule
CF = cash flow

With the cash flow statement complete, we can finally balance the balance sheet by adding the net change in cash to the prior-year cash balance to equal the current-year value. Net change in cash is calculated by summing operating cash flow, investing cash flow and financing cash flow. Finalising the balance sheet is a key moment of truth, as if you have made a mistake, then assets will not equal equity plus debt, and you will know that there is an incorrect or missing formula. Common errors include balance sheet item changes not flowing through to the cash flow statement, and failure to adjust the positive/negative sign on an equation when required.

Summary

When valuing a company, developing a full model to forecast forward financial statements is not a required step. However, it does add considerable rigour and detail to otherwise clunky guesstimates. There are four key steps to developing a model: prepare the financial statements, create assumptions, develop the supporting schedule, and then finally input equations that will drive the three financial statement outputs. If the correct steps are followed, the easiest way of checking that the links are broadly correct is to make sure that the balance sheet balances – that is, assets are equal to equity plus liabilities.

Accounting for Risk

Prudence is not avoiding danger, but calculating risk and acting decisively. Make mistakes of ambition and not mistakes of sloth – Niccolo Machiavelli

Do you work for free? The answer is probably not. You likely receive a salary in return for your labour. The same should be the case with money – when put to work, that should be compensated for with a return. Making money work for you, however, is more than a simple fortune cookie maxim. After the return calculation, it forms the second key component to a company's valuation – its required return.

In this chapter, we will quantify what that required return should be, based upon the judgements of a 'rational investor'. There are two key constituent parts to this required return: the opportunity cost (a risk-free investment forgone) and a risk premium to compensate for risk.

Required return = Opportunity cost + Risk premium

While the chapter introduces some maths, there is nothing that will not be explained, and it is all grounded in common sense. Ultimately, it comes down to asking yourself the following question: as a minimum, what percentage return should I objectively expect from an investment?

The opportunity cost

An opportunity cost is the loss of a potential gain or benefit when a certain choice is made. In practice, because our resources are limited, we are constantly making decisions and forgoing opportunities. For example, if you decide to have pizza rather than pasta for lunch, your opportunity cost in this instance is pasta – the choice forgone.

Opportunity cost is an important consideration for an investor, as if cash is being invested in an asset 'with risk', such as a share in a company, then the return on a risk-free asset is being forgone. For most of us, that would be leaving the cash in the bank and receiving interest. A key tenet of traditional finance theory however is that companies are valued by 'rational investors' – ones that are always seeking the absolute highest return per unit of risk. In this instance, the assumption would therefore be that rather than leave the cash in the bank it should instead be invested in the local currency government bond of the country in which the company operates. Relative to a bank deposit, a local government bond is also considered risk free, but offers a higher return and is therefore preferable.

This means one's absolute minimum required return for investing in any asset with risk should be in excess of a risk-free return – the government bond. Information on the return for government bonds in different geographies can be easily attained via the internet, by Googling '10-year government bond' and inputting the relevant country name. The next chart is a snapshot from tradingeconomics.com of what yield government bonds offered in late 2020.

Country	Yield
Brazil	7.5%
India	5.9%
Mexico	5.8%
US	0.9%
Australia	0.9%
New Zealand	0.9%
Canada	0.7%
UK	0.4%

There are two common questions that arise when using the 10-year bond. The first concerns whether a government bond is really 'risk free' – default being a particular concern when investing in emerging markets with fragile economies. While default is indeed technically a risk, during historic periods of financial stress, policy makers have typically opted to print more money rather than default on local currency obligations. This explains why, for example, excessive inflation has plagued countries such as Argentina during bouts of weakness.

The second common question concerns why we should use a 10-year bond, rather than one of a different maturity. The answer to this is that it is assumed that the target company being valued will operate into perpetuity (forever) and that a long-term investment will therefore match this long-term horizon (albeit imperfectly). The 10-year bond is selected as it is the longest duration bond that is issued across most economies, information on it is easily attainable and it is regularly traded ('liquid'), making it a reasonable proxy for long-term returns.

Risk premium

With the opportunity cost now calculated for, the risk premium needs to be incorporated. That is, how much more should an investor require above the government bond return as risk compensation? Absolutely no company is 'risk free', and therefore this is a relevant consideration no matter the valuation target. To determine the risk premium, we need to come back to a concept touched on at the start of the book – the distinction between company and market risk. Company risk refers to specific risks to a company, such as market share loss, a failed product launch or lawsuit. Meanwhile, market risk, otherwise known as systemic risk, incorporates events that affect all companies ('the market'). These might include the economy, a war, recession or natural disaster, and are sometimes referred to as 'systemic risks'.

All companies will have an element of both company and market risk, although the balance between the two can vary. For example, a bank is likely to have proportionately more market risk than a healthcare firm but is probably less exposed to company risk. That is not to say that a healthcare company by itself is any less risky, only that its outlook is less dependent on market factors such as the economy.

At this point we will make a rather big assumption – that a rational investor will seek to entirely eliminate company risk. Achieving this is simple enough. The rational investor would fully diversify his or her holdings so that no single position would meaningfully contribute or detract from the overall portfolio return. For example, if the investor had $1,000 to invest, that money would be invested across the stock market, rather than in any one individual company. The benefit of doing this is that the investor would then only be exposed to market risk. The drawback is that there would then be no opportunity to benefit from company-specific returns. While in theory full diversification means holding all companies, in practice the majority of risk reduction benefits from diversification are evident in a 30-stock portfolio. There are further risk benefits thereafter, but these are far more marginal.

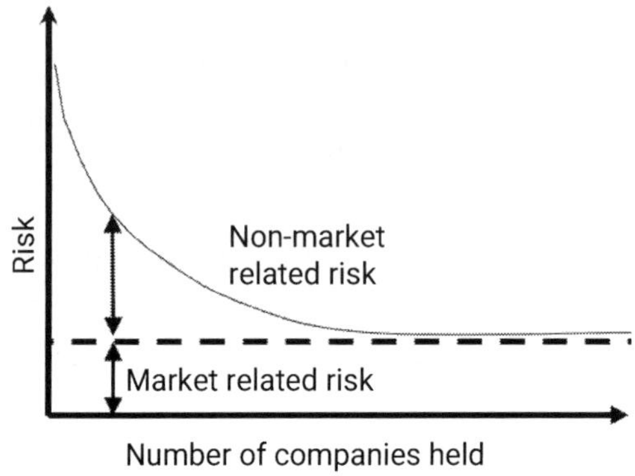

Full diversification to eliminate company risk is assumed desirable for a rational investor for two reasons. First, as traditional finance theory assume markets are efficient – price always equals value. Second, and more importantly, as diversification mathematically optimises the level of return per unit of risk. This second point may sound odd to start with, but risks are not additive if they are not entirely correlated. For instance, if you flip a coin and bet on both heads and tails, your risk has not doubled, as the two outcomes are not entirely correlated (indeed, in this instance they are entirely uncorrelated and your risk would be zero).

Similarly with companies, the relationship between any two firms will not be entirely linear, and there are therefore risk-reduction benefits to not 'putting all your eggs in one basket'. Due to this, a diversified portfolio will achieve the weighted return of its holdings, but less than the weighted risk of those same positions. The return per unit of risk rises. It is therefore technically preferable for a rational investor to hold the market portfolio (all stocks) and manage risk by either using leverage (higher risk) or allocating more to risk-free debt (lower risk).

The outcome of all this is that our 'rational investor' is fully diversified and is therefore only affected by market risk, as all company risk has now been diversified away. The question, therefore, is what should an investor at a minimum expect in return for being diversified and investing across the market? There are various ways to answer that, but typically it is done by looking at the long-term return of the market over decades. This is based on the premise that to understand what represents a reasonable expectation of returns going forward, we need to understand what they have been in the past. This varies greatly over time and market. However, when it is broken down into the market return in excess of the risk free rate (the government bond), that is generally found to be 3.5% to 5.5%. This is known as the risk premium.

Risk premium = Expected market return – Risk-free rate

For the sake of simplicity, we will use 5% in the following examples. In other words, the total return from investing in any equity markets should be five percentage points in excess of the risk-free rate to justify an investment in the market portfolio.

Required return = Risk-free rate + Risk premium

So, if in the US the risk-free rate were 1%, the required return would be 6% (1% + 5% = 6%). Alternatively, if the risk-free rate were 6% and the risk premium 5%, the required return would be 11% (6% + 5% = 11%). In some nations where economic development has lagged significantly – known as frontier markets – there are even some instances where the risk-free rate is as a high as 18% and therefore the required return around 23% (18% + 5% = 23%). Remember, the principle here is that a rational investor dislikes the uncertainty of the equity market and therefore needs to be compensated. Anything less than the required return would be unattractive, while anything more would be a great opportunity.

ADJUSTING THE RISK PREMIUM FOR A SPECIFIC COMPANY

While this is all nice in principle, it is of course a company that we want to value, and not all companies are equally exposed to market risk. As noted before, a bank, for example, would carry far more market risk than a healthcare company, due to its inherent cyclicality. Therefore, adjustments are needed to reflect this. This is achieved by adjusting the risk premium by the 'beta' (β) of the specific company being valued. The beta of a company is a standardised measure of its volatility relative to the overall economy. If a company had a beta of zero, that would indicate it was in no way correlated with the market. In other words, the two are utterly unrelated, and – much like it raining and you winning the lottery – one does not impact the other. Anything higher than zero then means that it is positively related (a rise in one will equal a rise in the other), while anything lower than zero means that it is negatively related (a rise in one would create a drop in the other).

Beta	Exposure	Examples
$\beta > 1$	More volatile than the market	Financials
$\beta = 1$	As volatile as the market	Consumer
$\beta < 1$	Less volatile than the market	Telecom
$\beta = 0$	Uncorrelated with the market	Lottery ticket
$\beta < 0$	Negatively correlated with the market	Gold miner

The above sector examples are very broad categorisations that companies in a certain sector typically fit into, but of course not all companies do. The beta of a company in the past is typically used as a reference for the beta it will have in the future. If, for example, the beta used was 1.2, that would suggest the company was expected to return 120% of what the market would return going forward (higher losses/gains). If the beta was only 0.7, the expectation would be that the company's return would be only 70% that of the expected market return (lower losses/gains). So in the event that the market rose 10%, in the first case the expected return would be 12% (120% × 10% = 12%), while in the latter case it would be 7% (70% × 10% = 7%).

For publicly listed companies, beta is typically calculated by using the historic share price return relationship of the target company with the broader market. It is calculated by dividing the covariance between the company and market return by the variance of the market.

$$\beta = \frac{\text{Covariance between the company and the market}}{\text{Variance of the market}}$$

Covariance is an unstandardised version of correlation that measures how two asset prices move together – their share price relationship. Variance, meanwhile, is a measure of volatility, determined by calculating the asset's return dispersion relative to its mean (the higher this is, the more volatile the asset). The details behind this are quite complex and require plenty of historical return data. Fortunately, the output to this equation is readily available online for most listed companies, and therefore very few try and calculate it themselves.

As a handful of examples, drawn from Yahoo Finance at the time of writing, the beta of Citigroup was 1.8, while those of Goldman Sachs, China Mobile and AstraZenica were 1.4, 0.7 and 0.3, respectively. These examples are based on the monthly relationship between the market and a stock over a period of five years, and these betas are typically quite stable across time.

While the beta found on these websites is an excellent starting point, it is worth applying some common sense if you think that a beta under or overstates a company's relationship with the broader equity market. For unlisted companies, a publicly listed peer is typically found and the beta of that peer used as a proxy, with minor adjustments made if required.

Required return to equity

With the risk-free rate, beta and risk premium all now established, we can now solve for what a rational investor's required return should be when investing in a given company. This is determined by using the capital asset price model (CAPM). This calculates the required return for equity by taking the opportunity cost (the risk-free rate) and adding the market risk premium, adjusted for the company-specific beta.

$$\text{Required return} = \text{Risk-free rate} + (\beta \times \text{Risk premium})$$

For example, in the case of Goldman Sachs, if the beta is 1.8, the 10-year government bond in the US is 0.91% and the market risk premium is presumed to be 5%, this would calculate to a required return of 9.9%.

$$9.9\% = 0.9\% + (1.8 \times 5\%)$$

We can therefore surmise that a rational investor would be indifferent between either investing in a US 10-year government bond and receiving the risk-free return of 0.91%, or taking a position in Goldman Sachs and receiving an 9.9% return. In risk-adjusted terms, both are equally attractive. To put this another way, if we expected that the annual total return received by investing in Goldman Sachs was anything in excess of 9.9%, then it would represent an attractive investment opportunity. Anything lower than 9.9% would suggest the level of return would not justify an investment. This point can be illustrated using the security market line, a representation of what the expected return given the risk should be. Anything then above the line would represent an attractive investment (a high expected return given the risk), while anything below would be unattractive (a low expected return given the risk). In the case of Goldman Sachs, 9.9% would place it exactly on the line.

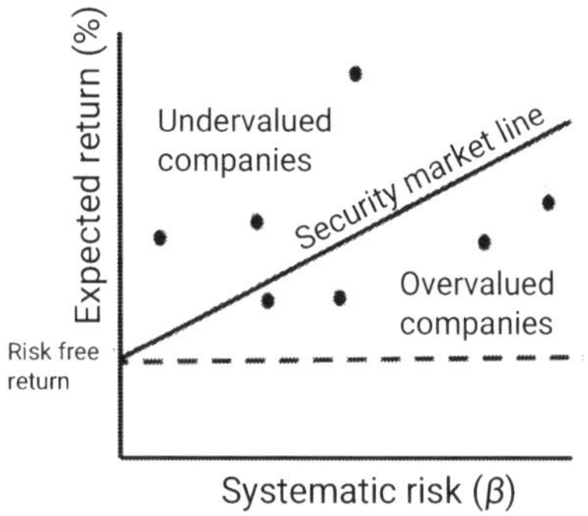

The required return on an investment is also frequently referred to as the cost of equity. This simply reflects that what a shareholder 'requires' for an investment will also represent the 'cost' of equity funding for a company. Using the previous example, if Goldman Sachs were to raise capital to grow, then 9.9% would be its cost of equity.

The weighted average required return to the firm

The required return on equity is of practical relevance to an investor and will be covered more fully in the following chapter. However, it can be further developed to reflect the required return for a company overall, including both debt and equity. This is known as the 'weighted average cost of capital', and it is the input of choice when valuing the 'firm value' rather than just the equity value. Fortunately, with equity already calculated for, the post-tax cost of debt and the capital structure weightings are the only other inputs required.

The cost of debt is nearly always less than the cost of equity, as it represents a fixed claim on cash flows and is higher up the capital structure in the event that the company collapses (liquidation). It is lower risk, and therefore the required return is lower. It can be determined by first calculating the effective interest rate on the company's debt, which can be found by dividing the current-year interest expense by total balance sheet debt. Use the average debt between the current and former year to avoid capturing only a year-end snapshot.

$$\text{Interest rate} = \frac{\text{Interest expense}}{\text{Average total debt}}$$

For example, if a company in 2020 had an interest expense of \$5 million, and the debt balance in the prior and current year had been \$90 million and \$110 million respectively, the effective interest rate would be 5% (\$100 million ÷ \$5 million = 5%).

The second step to calculating the cost of debt is to adjust it for the tax-reduction benefit that comes with being a pre-tax expense. This makes debt funding a highly tax-efficient form of funding, as it reduces taxes paid. To reflect this tax benefit, the cost of debt is multiplied by one minus the company's effective tax rate to produce a post-tax figure. For example, if the cost of debt was 5% pre-adjustment, and the corporate tax rate was 20%, the post-tax cost of debt would be 4% (5% × (1 – 20%) = 4%).

$$\text{Cost of debt} = \text{Interest rate} \times (1 - \text{Tax rate})$$

In the event that the company has bonds issued and trading, the effective interest rate on these will be a preferable representation of what the current required return is for debt investors. Indeed, even if a company does not have an outstanding bond, it is worth being aware about recent debt market movements of similar companies with outstanding bond issuances, so that adjustments can be made if rates have materially fluctuated.

Once the cost of debt and cost of equity have been calculated for, the weighting between debt funding and equity funding requires quantifying. This is calculated by dividing each funding source by total funding. For example, if a company had a total capital (debt and equity) of $100 million, and $30 million of that was debt while $70 million was equity, the capital structure would be said to be 30% debt and 70% equity.

Debt weight = 30% = $30 million ÷ $100 million

Equity weight = 70% = $70 million ÷ $100 million

With weights, cost of equity and post-tax cost of debt all known, the weighted average cost of capital can be determined. This is calculated by multiplying the cost of equity and post-tax debt by their respective weights, and then summing the outcome.

WACC = (% Equity)(Cost of equity) + (% Debt)(Post-tax cost of debt)

The WACC is a highly relevant figure, not just for the purpose of valuation but as a figure that should also feature in management discussions when new projects or investment opportunities with similar risks and financing structures are being considered. Just as a rational investor would not invest in a company priced with an expected return below the required return on equity, so too should a company's management not invest in opportunities where the expected return is below the required return for the firm (its WACC). As this is an important bellwether to assess value creation, getting the right capital structure for management becomes very important. In theory, management should use as much debt funding as possible, as interest is tax deductible and the cost of debt is lower than that of equity. In practice however, the more debt that is added to the structure, the higher the cost of both debt and equity, as more debt increases risk, which in turn increases the risk premium. There is therefore a balance to be found between making use of debt funding and not employing it excessively.

Summary

While the return profile of a company is most commonly commented on, its risk profile can dramatically affect how those returns are valued. For the purpose of valuation, risk is quantified as a percentage figure reflecting the minimum a rational investor should require in return for an investment. This includes both an opportunity cost component to reflect a risk-free investment forgone, and a risk premium to reflect compensation for market risk. Once the required return has been calculated, the interest rate on any outstanding debt can be incorporated to also calculate for the weighted cost of capital.

PRICE

Intrinsic Valuation

'Revenue is vanity, profit is sanity, but cash flow is king'

Performing an intrinsic valuation is where the rubber really meets the road, and all the risk and return assumptions get transformed into a single figure – the company's value. Intrinsic valuation boils a company down to its core reason for existence – to provide an actual return to shareholders. For all the pomp and fanfare that surrounds a company, if it does not achieve this, then it is without value. It's that simple.

Intrinsic valuation covers a number of valuation methods that calculate value from the bottom up, but in most instances it refers to the discounted cash flow model (indeed, most use the two names synonymously). Building a discounted cash flow model to determine the present value of that return is a three-part process. First, define what you mean by 'return' and pull in data from the cash flow projections. Second, adjust each cash flow to reflect the 'required return' covered in the last chapter. Finally, the cash flows need to be summed for the company's 'present value', otherwise known as its 'fair value' or 'intrinsic value' – what it is 'worth'. From here, the per share value can also be determined by dividing the intrinsic value by the number of outstanding shares.

For those who have developed a financial model, data will be pulled in from the financial statement projections, and it is advisable to include the valuation section below the financial model to avoid errors that might otherwise occur jumping between spreadsheets. There will be two key sections to an intrinsic valuation – the assumptions and the model itself. As per the financial model, keep to the same colour coding scheme when identifying between hard coded inputs (assumptions) and formula-driven cells (output).

Calculate the cash flows

The first step to creating a discounted cash flow model is to determine the measure of cash return that will be used as a return input. Is it cash in your pocket in the form of dividends, free cash flow to equity as a whole (FCFE), or free cash flow simply to the firm (FCFF)? A case can be made for each, as they all have benefits and weaknesses.

Cash flow	Calculation	Required return
Dividends	= Profit × Payout ratio	Cost of equity
FCFE	= CFO - CAPEX + Net debt issued	Cost of equity
FCFF	= CFO + (IE × (1 - TR)) - CAPEX	WACC

CFO: Cash Flow from Operations. IE: Interest Expense. TR: Tax Rate. Net debt: Debt minus Cash. WACC: Weighted Average Cost of Capital

The dividend is the most conservative and tangible cash flow input for calculating return. It is useful for companies that have a predictable dividend payout strategy, and is therefore typically applied to more mature companies. These often include banks, large oil and gas companies, and utilities. Its weakness is that the timing and scale of dividends from growth companies is hard to predict, and therefore it is generally avoided as the cash flow of choice for less mature or high-growth sectors like online services.

Cash flow to equity is the most intuitively relevant input, as it utilises cash direct to shareholders. This is calculated by taking annual cash flow from operations (CFO), subtracting annual capital expenditure (CAPEX), and adding annual net debt issued. It's a solid method for companies without complicated debt structures, but as soon as debt does become a material factor, it runs the risk of significant estimation error, as cash flows from debt issuance or repayment can be large and substantially influence the end output. This is therefore most commonly used as a means of valuation for companies with limited debt.

The final possible cash return input is free cash flow to the firm. This is the most broadly used and generally recommended – so if in any doubt, use this one. It is calculated as cash flow from operations, plus adjusted interest expense, minus capital expenditure. The benefit of using this cash flow as an input is that it can be applied consistently across all types of company, no matter the payout ratio or volatility in debt issuance. However, as the cash flow is to the firm (both debt and equity), there are two further adjustments required:

- Debt will need to be subtracted from the end output to determine the underlying equity value (equity = assets – debt).
- A weighted discount rate that incorporates both debt and equity will need to be applied – the WACC covered in the last chapter.

Adjust for risk

Cash might be king, but identical amounts do not equal identical value if the timing of receipt varies. For example, the anticipation of receiving $100 in a year will not please us as much as receiving $100 today. This is for reasons described in the last chapter – opportunity cost and risk. Cash has what is known as 'time value', and a return should therefore be required for waiting – the 'required return'. To capture this in a company's cash flows, the required return is used as the discount rate, to discount all future cash flows to a 'present value', as demonstrated in the equation below.

$$\text{Present value} = \sum \frac{\text{Future Value}}{(1 + \text{Discount rate})^n}$$

This equation may look intimidating, but we will unbundle it into three parts: present value, the exponent and the sum. First, the 'present value'. This takes a future value and discounts it to down to a value that, given the required return, a rational individual would be equally content to receive. It is calculated as the future value of the cash flow divided by one plus the discount rate. For example, if you expected to receive \$100 in a year's time and your required return on that cash flow was 5%, that would equal a present value of \$95.

$$\text{Present value} = \$95 = \frac{\$100}{(1 + 0.05)}$$

\$100 in a year, or \$95 today – different numbers, but to a rational individual both propositions would be equally attractive given the 5% required return. Notably, the higher the required return, the less the present value of the future cash flow. For example, if instead of remaining at 5% the risk increased to 10%, the present value would drop to \$91, as the recipient would become even keener to receive cash today rather than waiting.

This analysis is fine for a financial asset with a single cash flow one year ahead, but a company's cash flows will stretch well beyond that. This is why in the equation there is an exponent labelled 'n' above the bracketed one plus required return. The n stands for 'number of years' and should be equal to the number of years that the cash flow is being discounted back to its present value. The result is that it compounds the base (1+r) by 'n' years. So, if the discount rate were 5%, for example:

Year	Exponent	Equivalent calculation	Output
Year 1	1.05^1	1.05	1.05
Year 2	1.05^2	1.05 × 1.05	1.10
Year 3	1.05^3	1.05 × 1.05 × 1.05	1.16
Year 4	1.05^4	1.05 × 1.05 × 1.05 × 1.05	1.21

This step is to tailor the required return to the period of each individual cash flow. The longer an investor has to wait, the greater the required return, the heavier the discount to a cash flow, and consequently the lower its present value.

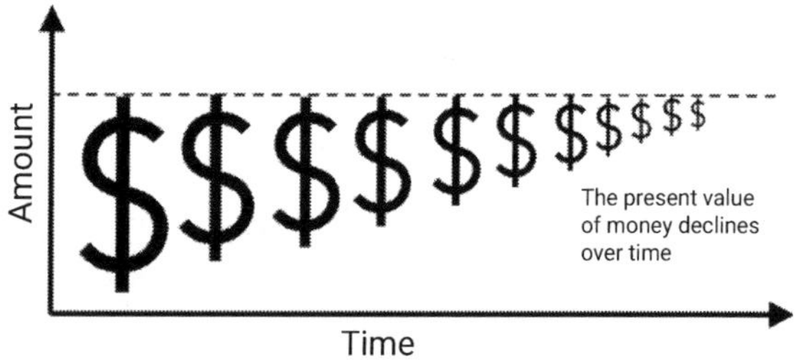

So, \$100 today, \$95 in a year (\$100 ÷ 1.05 = \$95) or \$82 in four years (\$100 ÷ 1.21 = \$82) – all would have the same present value to a rational individual, assuming a 5% discount rate.

Year	Calculation	Present value
Year 1	$=\$100 \div (1+0.05)^1$	\$95
Year 2	$=\$100 \div (1+0.05)^2$	\$91
Year 3	$=\$100 \div (1+0.05)^3$	\$86
Year 4	$=\$100 \div (1+0.05)^4$	\$82

The final component to the equation, is the Σ (sigma). This is simply a Greek capital letter used to represent 'the sum' – a mathematical shorthand for long lists of additions. In the case of the equation, it is an instruction to add together every discounted cash flow, no matter if it's $10 in a year or $10 million in a thousand years from now.

$$\text{Present value} = \frac{\text{Cash flow}}{(1+R)^n} + \frac{\text{Cash flow}}{(1+R)^n} + \frac{\text{Cash flow}}{(1+R)^n} \ldots$$

Put principles into practice

The key message of this chapter is that a company's value is based on its collective risk-adjusted cash flows. However, this does not mean that we will model and adjust each of those into perpetuity. You probably don't have the time, Excel certainly does not have enough cells and, most importantly, projections quickly become more and more erroneous as a time frame extends out. Instead, we can cheat. This is done by breaking a company's cash flows into two parts: near-term interim cash flows and a final terminal cash flow.

$$\text{Value} = \text{Interim cash flows} + \text{Terminal value}$$

Interim cash flows are those that have been modelled in the financial statements – typically three to five years forward. Ideally, these will be calculated up until a point when the company matures and growth stabilises to a sustainable rate. In the case of the terminal value, this is best thought of as the value that the company could be sold at, come the end of the interim period – so a final cash payment which reflects all future value beyond that point.

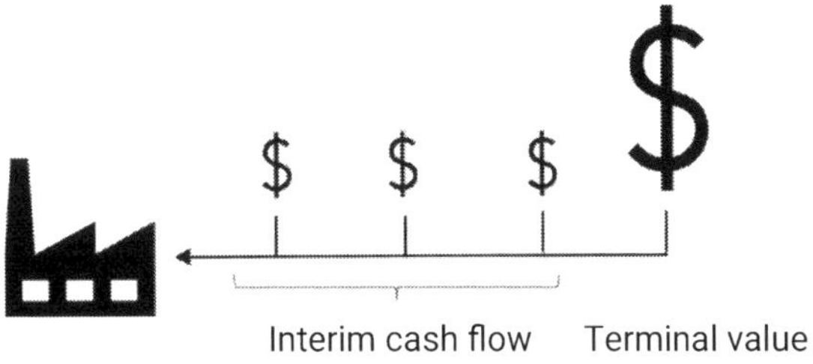

The terminal value is calculated using either the perpetual growth method or, if the company is still in a high growth phase, an exit multiple. The perpetual growth method is a mathematical means of discounting all future cash flows into a single final value, given a certain growth and discount rate. This is done by taking the final cash flow, growing it one year by the sustainable growth rate (g), and then dividing it by the discount rate (r) minus the sustainable growth rate.

$$\text{Terminal Value} = \frac{\text{Cash flow } (1 + g)}{r - g}$$

If by some means you could value cash flows into perpetuity using the sustainable growth rate, the terminal value would be your output. It is therefore a very neat means of simplifying the model. It is however highly influenced by the sustainable growth rate assumption. This will always be a very approximate guess, normally based around a long-term GDP prediction – but advisably lower, as no company can grow in excess of GDP forever and the law of large numbers works against larger firms.

Notably, if you already believe that the company you are assessing has reached maturity and stability, and you want to avoid the hassle of creating a financial model, the most current full-year cash flow can be used as the input, with the terminal value then becoming the present value. This can sometimes be the case for telecom or utility companies.

For instance, if a water utility produced $30 million of dividends in 2020, was expected to grow 2% annually and the discount rate (required return) was 5%, that would equal a current value of just over $1 billion. In this case, as dividends are used as the return, that $1 billion would be the company's 'fair' value.

$$\$1.02 \text{ billion} = \frac{\$30 \text{ million} \times (1 + 2\%)}{(5\% - 2\%)}$$

The challenge arises when a company is still many years from reaching a mature growth phase, for instance Amazon or Facebook. This is typically dealt with by using an exit multiple. The exit multiple uses relative valuation to surmise what the company should be worth in that final forecast year – ie what value it could be 'exited' at if it were sold.

Relative valuation is covered in detail in the next chapter. When applying it to intrinsic valuation however, the enterprise value to EBITDA ratio is the most commonly selected multiple of choice when dealing with cash flow to the firm. Alternatively, if dividends or cash flow to equity are the return input, then the price to earnings or price to sales are frequently used. These valuation ratios will all be covered in detail come the next chapter. While using an exit multiple might not be as mathematically watertight as using a sustainable growth rate, it is widely used by industry professionals.

For an analyst who has used either dividends or free cash flow to equity as the return input, the process stops here. The present value of the discounted cash flows (both interim and terminal) is equal to market value. However, if the input to the model was free cash flow to the firm, then the discounted cash flow value output would be equal to its enterprise value (equity plus net debt). To therefore solve for equity value alone, the net debt would need to be subtracted – net debt is equal to total debt minus cash and cash equivalents.

$$\text{Enterprise value} = \text{Equity value} + \text{Net debt}$$

$$\text{Equity Value} = \text{Enterprise value} - \text{Net debt}$$

Finally, no matter how the company's equity value has been determined, if beyond the value of the company you want to attain the per share value, then divide the company's calculated value by the current number of outstanding shares (found in the most recent financial statements).

$$\text{Per share Value} = \frac{\text{Equity value}}{\text{Total outstanding number of shares}}$$

If the purpose of the valuation is to ascertain whether an investment in a company represents an attractive investment opportunity, the share price calculated can then be compared to the current share price to inform an opinion. If intrinsic value is higher than the share price, the company is undervalued and a share purchase would be accretive. If it is lower than the share price, an investment would be unattractive. The greater the differential between the intrinsic value and price, the greater the upside/downside to an investment.

Summary

Intrinsic valuation nearly always refers to the discounted cash flow model. This model can use a number of different input combinations, although using free cash flows to the firm and the company's weighted average cost of capital is the most common. The key steps are to discount all of a company's cash flows and then subtract debt. However, because incorporating all of a company's cash flows is impractical, for brevity's sake only near-term company cash flows are included, and then a terminal value is assumed, to mathematically reflect all future flows beyond that point. If the per share value of the company is then sought, divide the calculated intrinsic value of the company by the number of outstanding shares to conclude on a 'fair price'. For those investing, any price higher than the calculated fair price would suggest that the company was overvalued (not worth buying), while anything lower would imply it was undervalued (attractive).

Relative Valuation

'Everything is relative; and only that is absolute' – Auguste Comte

The French philosopher Auguste Comte famously wrote 'everything is relative; and only that is absolute'. A similar underlying principle can be applied to the valuation process, resulting in an approach known as relative valuation. Relative valuation is the practice of using one asset to determine the value of another. It is the most broadly used means of calculating a company's worth.

This concept of course will not be unfamiliar. When transacting in anything – be it a fridge or car – our judgement of what is a reasonable price to pay will be based to some extent on comparable transactions in that product. You would not, for instance, likely agree to pay $1 million for a property if a similar one two doors away had just sold for $500,000. People want a bargain, and to pay less for more. So too with a rational investor.

Not every good or company however may be of equal size. This is, for example, why estate agents often talk about property value in terms of price per square foot, rather than referencing an absolute value. Similarly, alcoholic drinks are required to report on % ABV (alcohol by volume), and most food products will list ingredients such as sugar per 100g. In each instance, the values have been standardised so that they are readily comparable against alternatives.

With a company too, it is highly unlikely there will be a similar peer equivalent in terms of size and profitability. Therefore, a measure of price per unit of performance or position can be determined to standardise 'value'. This is achieved by dividing the company's market value (its 'price') by a financial statement item such as sales or profit to create a price per unit ratio, otherwise known as a multiple.

$$\text{Multiple} = \frac{\text{Price}}{\text{Financial statement item}}$$

This multiple makes any company, no matter the size, comparable to its peers. Therefore, peer multiples can be used to determine the price of the target company to be valued. This is achieved by multiplying the average multiple at which its peers trade with the financial statement that has been input.

$$\text{Company value} = \text{Financial statement item} \times \text{Peer average multiple}$$

For example, if peers traded at a calculated average multiple of three times sales, and the company being valued had $30 million of sales, its value would be $90 million (3 × $30 million × $30 million = $90 million).

Peers

Company	Sales	Value	Multiple
A	$10 million	$3 million	3.3x
B	$3 million	$1 million	3x
C	$100 million	$38 million	2.6x
Average			3x

Target company

Company	Sales	Multiple	Value
A	$30 million	3x	$90 million

As with intrinsic valuation, if from that $90 million valuation you wanted to determine the price per share, a final step would be dividing the value by the number of shares outstanding. For example, if there were 45 million shares outstanding, then the price per share in the above example would be \$2 (\$90 million ÷ 45 million = \$2).

Notably, while this is a means of valuing a company, in practice if the purpose is to invest in a company, different opportunities will simply be compared based on their multiple. For example, if two similar companies named A and B traded at 15x and 10x respectively, you would buy B in the expectation that the valuation would re-rate upwards to the same level as A, 15x. In this instance, the valuation re-rating would equal a 50% return (15 ÷ 10 - 1 = 50%). As per the case with intrinsic valuation, the assumption is that markets should be efficient and there technically should be no scope to arbitrage (ie no 'free lunch' when it comes to a mispriced company).

While the basic principle behind relative valuation may be simple, there are three key variables that must be decided on when applying it to a company: the peer group selected, the period selected and, most importantly, the ratio selected. At this point, there is not a one-size-fits-all standard, and judgements will be required on how to frame the ratio in a way that provides a robust valuation output.

Period group

As a company's earnings are unlikely to be static over time, any relative valuation determination will require consideration of what period the financial statement figure is lifted from – historic, trailing or projected. Historic refers to the past full year, trailing refers to the past 12 months (so, the last four quarters or last two halves) and projected is based on a forecast future figure.

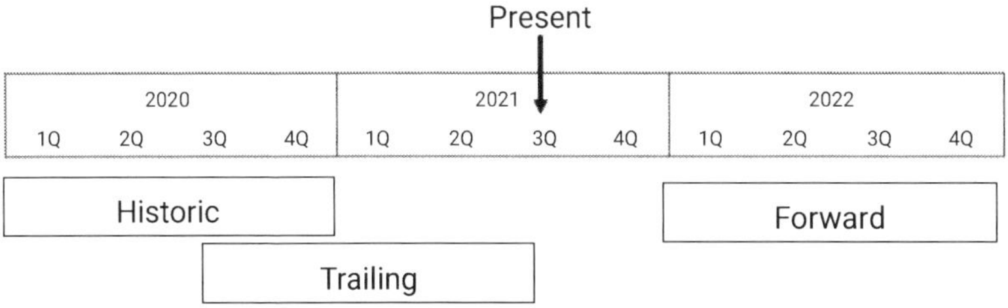

The most commonly used amongst individual investors is the trailing 12-month multiple, (the 'TTM'). Benefits include that most financial websites display this multiple, it does not require making any projections, it reflects recent performance, and there is no forecast error. The key weakness is that during abnormal periods for the company or economy, such as a product recall or recession, there is a risk that the output will severely under- or over-state value, unless seriously heavily adjustments are made. For this reason, professional investors such as asset managers, who have easy access to forward projections across a broad range of companies, will often select a period one or two years in the future that normalises out abnormal activity.

Whichever period is selected, it is important to use it consistently across all peers so that the ratio is adequately comparable. This is especially true when near-term growth estimates vary across a peer group.

Peers

The second important consideration is peer group. Institutional investors will often lean on index providers such as MSCI or FTSE to provide sector or industry peers for a company. Individuals, meanwhile, can reference online financial sites, such as Google Finance, which do a reasonable job of breaking out a company's comparable peers. For example, in the case of Heineken, Google Finance lists Carlsberg, Anheuser-Busch InBev and Coca-Cola as peers. Importantly, the peer group should be comparable enough that companies have a similar risk/return profile, while also being broad enough that it can incorporate a range of companies. If there are a wide range of outcomes for your average, it's worth re-assessing if you have the correct peer companies or if there are specific reasons for the dispersion.

Once the peer group has been determined and an average ratio calculated, it will almost certainly require adjusting up or down, based on the strength or weakness of the company being valued relative to the peer group. This part is unfortunately not an exact science, and the degree to which this will be required will be based upon how comparable the peers are. A typical premium or discount adjustment, however, would normally be around 10% to 50%. If it is considerably more, the peer group may need reconsidering. For listed companies, the extent of any adjustment can be steered by the extent of the premium/discount at which the company has traded relative to peers historically. Be aware however that relationships between companies change over time, and therefore so does the valuation differential.

Beyond using a peer group average to determine what a relevant multiple should be for a company, the multiple can also be based on the trading history of a company's shares. Charts for this can be found online. As a very simple example, if a company had in the past traded on average at 10x, then that would be the assumed current fair value multiple for the purpose of valuation.

The key question then becomes over what period is the 'average' assessed. Too short and it risks not fully incorporating a company's full range of lows/highs. Too long and it risks becoming dated. Typically, a three- to five-year average is used, but a longer period can be longer for more mature and stable companies. As with peer valuation, adjustments will almost certainly be needed as the risk/return profile of a company changes over time.

The key ratios

There are a number of different financial statement inputs that can be used when calculating a company's valuation ratio. Each have their relative strengths and weaknesses, and some are more appropriate to certain types of company than others. Typically, however, an individual will assess a company across a range of measures and time periods, and against its peers and its own history, to ensure any conclusion is robust.

Below is an example of a valuation table, the ratio calculations for which can be all be found online for listed companies.

	Price to earnings	EV to EBITDA	Dividend yield	Free cash flow yield	Price to book
Company A	15x	5x	2%	4%	2.1x
Company B	9x	3x	4%	6%	1.2x
Company C	12x	4x	3%	3%	1.5x
Company D	13x	4x	2%	4%	1.6x
Average	12x	4x	3%	4%	1.6x

Price to earnings multiple

The price to earnings multiple is the most popular valuation ratio. It is calculated as price divided by earnings and is often simply referred to as the 'PE' or 'earnings multiple'.

$$\text{PE ratio} = \frac{\text{Price}}{\text{Earnings}}$$

The ratio quantifies how many times larger a company's value is relative to its earnings. So, if the multiple were 10x, for example, this would mean that the company's value was equal to ten times its earnings. Essentially, the higher the PE multiple, the higher the valuation of the company.

The key benefit of the PE multiple as a measure of relative value is that for many investors, earnings are the key measure of shareholder return, making them a practical anchor to tether valuation to. The weakness of the PE ratio is that if a company is not profitable, it is of no use, and if earnings are highly volatile, it becomes problematic.

This issue can be partly remedied by ensuring that the earnings used are normalised by exempting any one-off figures. For example, if a company recognised a gain on the sale of an asset, this would be best subtracted from the earnings figure as it is non-recurring. A further common-sense check to determine what is 'normal' would be to assess the company's margin over time and whether it has historically mean reverted. This will not be the case for all companies, but for those for which you can get a rough idea of a through-the-cycle average, this can be applied to sales to further normalise earnings.

One variation of the PE ratio is the PEG ratio, which provides a further means of standardising a company's valuation relative to peers by incorporating growth. It is calculated by dividing the PE ratio by earnings growth.

$$\text{PEG ratio} = \frac{\text{PE ratio}}{\text{Earnings growth}}$$

Just like the PE ratio, the earnings growth input can be historic, trailing or forward, and each option has its own benefits and weaknesses. In general, however, the forward estimated earnings growth input is most commonly used. Yahoo Finance, for instance, uses the five-year forward estimate as the input for its displayed PEG figure. There is no single perfect 'PEG' ratio, as it overlooks required return. However, it is a very helpful starting point for those scouring the equity market for opportunities worth doing further work on. It is used particularly often for high-growth companies such as online service firms, where the PE multiple is likely higher and the valuation dispersion amongst peers significant. In general, a PEG ratio of 1 is often perceived to be indicative of a fair multiple. Anything lower is often considered 'cheap', and anything higher, 'expensive'.

Price to sales multiple

Some of the key weaknesses of the PE multiple are solved with the price to sales (PS) multiple. To start with, it is nearly always a far less variable financial statement line than earnings, and this means it is far easier to determine a normalised level. This makes it particularly helpful during periods of economic stress or excess, when earnings can swing wildly and it may be difficult to develop or get hold of reasonable forward-looking estimates. Furthermore, as it does not incorporate the margin profile of a company, it is indifferent to the profitability of the target. This makes it particularly often used for less mature companies, where the margin is understated due to profits being reinvested into the business (for example, Amazon).

$$\text{Price to sales} = \frac{\text{Price}}{\text{Sales}}$$

Just like the price to earnings multiple, a company's price to sales can be assessed against peers or against its own history. The key weakness of this measure is that when compared against peers, it accounts for neither the operational profitability of the company or the capital structure. It is therefore very important that if you use a peer group average, you find peers with a similar long-term return profile.

EV/EBITDA multiple

A reasonable compromise between the PE and PS ratios is the EV to EBITDA ratio. It's not as volatile as earnings but does not overlook the company's margin entirely. It is calculated by dividing the company's enterprise value by its EBITDA (earnings before interest, tax, depreciation and amortisation.)

$$\text{EV/EBITDA multiple} = \frac{\text{Enterprise value}}{\text{EBITDA}}$$

There are two differences between this ratio and the PS and PE ratios. The first is that enterprise value is used instead of price – the distinction being that price is a company's market value, while enterprise value is a measure of a company's 'total value' (both its net debt and market value).

$$\text{Enterprise value} = \text{Market cap} + \text{Debt} - \text{Cash}$$

Effectively, enterprise value is what you would be liable to pay were you to buy a business outright – purchase the equity and pay off the net debt. This makes it a particularly practical measure of value for a company that is a takeover target, as it reflects the total cost of acquisition. Its weakness is that it is a less relevant means of value for simple equity ownership, which will be the primary concern of most equity investors.

The second difference is that EBTIDA is probably not a line that you will find in the income statement. It is calculated manually by taking the income statement EBIT (earnings before interest tax or 'operating profit'), then adding back cash flow statement depreciation and amortisation for that period.

$$\text{EBITDA} = \text{EBIT} + \text{Depreciation} + \text{Amortisation}$$

A company's EBITDA should be a reasonable representation of its pre-tax cash profits, and is therefore a robust measure of raw return. It is a particularly useful means of valuation for companies that are relatively stable operationally but which have volatile earnings due to fixed costs such as depreciation, amortisation and interest expenses. This is often the case with industrial companies, where non-cash charges are proportionately large and, as a consequence, earnings are often volatile.

The key weaknesses of the EV/EBITDA ratio is that it overlooks certain costs. These should therefore be considered when thinking about the premium or discount that it should trade at relative to peers. For example, how does its effective tax rate compare to peers? This can vary between geography. Also, how capital intensive is its business model? This will influence the level of reinvestment required in the company.

Dividend yield

Dividends are the most tangible form of return for an investor. Straight off the bat however, you will notice something different about this ratio – it is a yield rather than a multiple. The difference is that price is on the bottom (the denominator) rather than on the top (the numerator). The ratio is flipped.

$$\text{Dividend yield} = \frac{\text{Dividend}}{\text{Price}}$$

The consequence of this switch is that a lower yield implies the company is more expensive, and a higher one that it is less. For example, we would say that a company with a 5% dividend yield is cheaper than one with a dividend yield of 2%. The other consequence of flipping from a multiple to a yield is that to produce a company's value, the financial statement input (the dividend) is divided by the yield rather than multiplied by it.

$$\text{Company value} = \frac{\text{Dividend}}{\text{Dividend yield}}$$

The key strength of the dividend yield is that it informs an investor about the actual income return. This, when added with the growth rate assumption, will equal a shareholder's total return. For example, if a telecom company had a dividend yield of 4%, a stable payout and was expected to grow earnings consistently at 3%, the total annual return would be 7% (3% + 4% = 7%). This could then be compared against the required return, to determine if 7% was an attractive return (higher than what a rational investor should require) or unattractive (lower than the required return).

A further benefit of the dividend yield is that for many companies the dividend is less volatile than other financial line items such as earnings. This is because even during periods of economic weakness, management often tries to maintain a stable dividend if at all possible. For instance, until 2020, energy company Shell had not once cut its dividend since World War 2, despite plenty of ups and downs. The dividend yield is therefore often considered a comparatively stable measure of value. One weakness of the dividend yield is that many companies pay no dividend, so it is not applicable to all firms. Non-dividend payers include some of the largest names in the world, such as Amazon, Google and Facebook.

Free cash flow yield

The free cash flow yield is the other key yield ratio. This measure is based on free cash flow from the cash flow statement – calculated by taking operating cash flow and deducting capital expenditure. This is then divided by the market value of the company to transform it into a yield.

$$\text{Cash flow yield} = \frac{\text{Free cash flow}}{\text{Market value}}$$

The advantage of this ratio is that cash flow is harder to manipulate by management than earnings, and it represents the actual cash profitability of the company as a whole. The weakness is that without accrual adjustments, it can be very lumpy between periods, and therefore it is hard to determine a 'normalised level'. This is a particular issue for growth companies and those with long working capital cycles. As with dividends, therefore, it is often used for mature companies with stable growth prospects, such as utility and telecom firms.

Price to book multiple

Basing the company's value on its equity book value is the most intuitive method, as unlike the other measures, equity book value is itself a reasonable starting point for what a company's value might be. We are, after all, trying to find the fair value of a company's equity. The price to book multiple is calculated by dividing the market value of a company by its equity (found on the balance sheet).

$$\text{PB multiple} = \frac{\text{Market value}}{\text{Equity}}$$

Of course, for reasons detailed earlier, it is rarely the case that a company will trade at exactly its equity book value. This is largely due to intangible assets such as brand and research being expensed as incurred, rather than capitalised onto the balance sheet. We therefore still need to develop a peer and/or historical average to determine a fair value.

The price to book multiple is of most practical use for financial companies such as banks, insurance providers and property developers. The value of such companies is largely accounted for on the balance sheet, and a 'normalised' income statement or cash flow value may be hard to come by due to the volatility of these businesses. These companies will often trade at 0.5x to 2x price to book, although the average historic level for a given financial company can be volatile between periods.

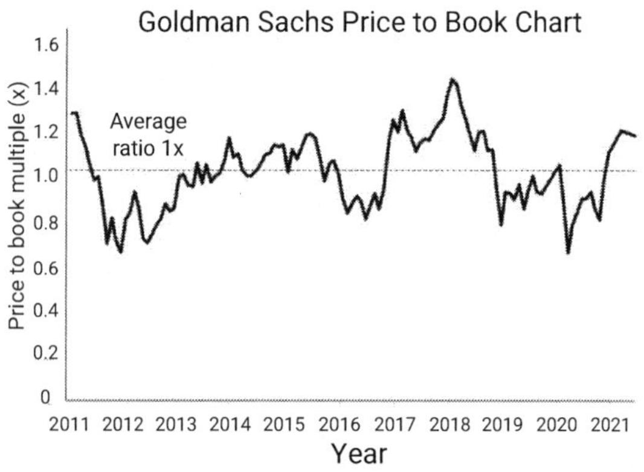

The key benefit of the PB multiple is that it is applicable irrespective of profitability (or lack thereof). This makes it a particularly practical multiple during periods of economic stress, when earnings might collapse but the valuation should not – remembering that a single year's earnings for a company is relatively negligible in the context of its overall value. As the PB multiple is anchored in the equity value, rather than a measure of performance such as sales or profits, it is also typically far more stable over time. This can make it easier to assess for comparative purposes, be it against a company's peers or its own history.

In terms of weaknesses, it is a very poor measure of value for companies with large off-balance 'assets' such as brand, customer base or intellectual property, or for those with high return growth opportunities. Amazon, for example, has in the past traded at over 15x its book value. Beyond this, inflation and technology change can create sizeable discrepancies between the market value and accounting value of some assets over time. Accounting standards of course make provision for any instance where an asset is worth more on the balance sheet than its value. However, judgements on these matters are subjective and can be influenced by management. It is therefore not uncommon for some companies to persistently trade at a discount to book value, especially when cash is being reinvested into low-return opportunities.

Alternative measures

Ultimately, for relative valuation, any measure could be used as an input. What's key is that it needs to be predictive in some way of future returns. While for Unilever that might be dividend yield, for Visa it might be price to earnings, and for Amazon it could be price to sales. An analyst is however not limited to the financial statements alone. For example, when Facebook bought WhatsApp in 2014 for $16 billion, WhatsApp was unprofitable across every measure, and even its sales were only a paltry $10.2 million the prior year. Facebook knew, however, that WhatsApp had a phenomenal economic moat and would be able to monetise users over time. Analysis was therefore based largely upon the price per user multiple (price divided by users). On this measure, Facebook managed to buy WhatsApp for 'only' $42 per user, when in contrast Twitter at the time was valued at around $150 per user, Facebook at $140 per user and LinkedIn at $120 per user.

While alternative inputs are helpful for companies where there is a risk that traditional financial metrics could under- or over-state true value relative to peers, the user should be careful to remember that ultimately any company will need to produce a return to have any value. Therefore, in the case of WhatsApp, whether it was purchased at $42 per user or $4 per user would be irrelevant if in the end it could not provide investors with a return.

A sum of the parts approach

For more complex companies that operate in multiple different markets, deciding on the right peer group or ratio to use can pose a dilemma. Take General Electric, for example. The company operates in markets from aviation and oil to renewables and healthcare – business segments with very different peer groups and appropriate ratios. This issue is typically dealt with by valuing the various business segments separately and then summing the parts up – hence the name 'sum of the parts'. Summing up the operating assets (business segments) of a company will equal a 'gross asset value' figure, equivalent to the enterprise value. From this point, equity value can be determined by subtracting net debt. When completing a SOTP valuation, the resulting equity value figure is often referred to as the 'net asset value', as a further premium/discount may be applied to reach a 'fair value'.

Business segment	Valuation method	Peer average	Value
Food segment	PE	15x	$50 million
Telecom segment	PS	2x	$20 million
Banking segment	PB	1.3x	$5 million
Gross asset value			$75 million
Net debt			$20 million
Net asset value (NAV)			$95 million

The inputs for the SOTP approach are typically found using the business segment breakdown in a company's financial statements, with the commentary in the management discussion section used to assess the prospects of each separate business unit. While this might sound simple, segment reporting categories are based on 'management's approach', which gives management quite wide discretion in terms of how each segment is defined. In addition, disclosure beyond the sales breakdown can be poor, therefore making a margin difficult to break out in order to perform ratios such as the EV/EBITDA ratio. To solve for this, cost allocation guesstimates often need to be employed.

It is frequently the case that larger companies with complex structures trade at a discount to their equity value on an ongoing basis. To give an example, the huge Japanese conglomerate Softbank has at points in the past traded at over a 50% discount to its sum of the parts value, despite large segments of the company's value being listed on an exchange (for instance, its stakes in Alibaba, Sprint and Yahoo Japan). For this reason, analysts sometimes apply a 'conglomerate discount' to any end valuation to reflect the practical reality that investors do not like the complications that come with complex companies and are frequently suspicious of management's capability to realise shareholder value. In such instances, value could be created by asset sales and simplification of the company, although unfortunately this is all too often not pursued. It is not unknown for companies to trade at a premium to their net asset value when management is highly regarded and trusted by investors to make wise value-creating capital allocation choices. It is rare, however.

Summary

Relative valuation is the most common means of determining a company's worth. While this does not offer the rigour of intrinsic valuation, it does benefit from being simple and easily understood. The key principle is that similar companies should trade at similar values, and therefore by using standardised measures of value (multiples and yields) a company's value can be attained. The most common relative valuation metric is the price to earnings multiple, although others measures, such as price to sales, EV/EBITDA, dividend yield, free cash flow yield and price to book, can be more applicable in certain situations.

SPECIAL VALUATION SITUATIONS

Mergers & Acquisitions

When thinking of investing, most people picture chaotic Wall Street trading floors packed with traders feverishly buying and selling shares in companies. However, investing activity encompasses a wide spectrum of styles, from the use of high-frequency trading algorithms, often involving the holding shares for no longer than a fraction of a second, to slow-moving pension funds seeking to buy and hold companies for the long term. Fortunately, the valuation methodology is the same in either case.

When, however, a transaction does impact upon the prospects of a company is when it is in the form of a merger or acquisition and a consolidation of companies or assets take place. In this instance, the financials of the companies involved need to not just be added together but also updated to reflect the deal structure and potential synergy benefits derived from the combination. To achieve this, an M&A model must be developed. The principal steps in an M&A model are no different to any other company valuation model, although additional considerations and adjustments are required.

The M&A process

Buying shares in a publicly listed company is simple – create an account, put on a buy order, and you will receive the shares at the price at which they are trading in the market. The M&A process is far more cumbersome, typically taking six months to a year to complete, and often requiring the services of lawyers, investment bankers and brokers to help facilitate the transaction.

The process articulated below is relevant to all M&A. However, while the term M&A refers to the consolidation of two companies, there are nuanced differences between a 'merger' and 'acquisition' in so far as a merger is a legal consolidation of two companies, whereas an acquisition is specifically when one entity takes ownership of another. There is also a distinction in terms of buyer, as the acquirer might be either financial or strategic. The former refers to purchases by an institutional investor, such as a private equity firm. The latter is typically undertaken by a company (often one operating in the same industry) that seeks to integrate the purchase into itself. For the purpose of process and valuation, the two are the same. In practice though, for a financial buyer, the synergies and stock consideration in any deal will normally be zero, unless the acquired company is merged with another portfolio company.

The initial step for a company seeking M&A is to develop an M&A strategy document that articulates the type of target being sought. Once a deal has been identified, initial contact should be made with a letter of intent (LOI) that expresses the potential acquirer's interest in pursuing a merger or acquisition and summarises a proposed deal. The LOI at this stage is very high level and details within are subject to change. These typically includes details of the proposed agreement, a target date for signing, preconditions, price range and any obligations of each party under the agreement. The LOI does not represent a legally binding contract in terms of the deal, although it may have legally binding terms. These could include a non-solicitation agreement to prevent poaching of employees or customers, an exclusivity provision that prevents parties from negotiating with others, and a confidentially agreement. In addition to getting a conversation started with the target company, the LOI is a helpful means of opening up the right channels to gain information that can be used in a financial analysis.

The next stage is for the acquirer to develop an M&A model and valuation. This should comprise a thorough financial assessment, including consideration of any likely operational and financial synergies. It's not uncommon to lean on the expertise of consultants and investment bankers at this stage. The output of the valuation model is then used to determine deal terms that can be presented to the target company. The acquirer will want to balance offering the lowest possible price with having a competitive offer on the table, and this often requires a period of negotiation. Ultimately, for both the acquirer and target, the deal needs to create shareholder value to be worth pursuing. Therefore, if it cannot be done at a valuation that is accretive, it should not be signed. If the buyer is a financial sponsor, the criterion for whether a deal is worth pursuing tends to be that the investment exceeds a targeted specific internal rate of return (IRR) within a specific timeframe. This will be covered within the LBO chapter.

Once a deal is finally agreed, accepted and signed (albeit non-binding), time and resources are committed to a thorough due diligence of the company in order to confirm or correct the buyer's assessment of the company. This stage typically takes a couple of months and involves a more exhaustive assessment of the business to ensure that everything is at it appears. While each deal is different, often a checklist approach is used to ensure that the process is comprehensive. Below is an example template for items that are commonly covered during due diligence.

1. Corporate structure
    - Incorporation documents
    - Corporate bylaws
    - Organisational chart
2. Shareholder matters
    - Lists of all securities holders
    - Stock option agreements and plans
    - Stockholder and voting agreements
3. Taxes
    - Tax returns filed in the last five years
    - Correspondence with tax authority

4. Strategic fit
    - Personnel and company culture
    - Integration and transition benefits/costs
5. Intellectual property
    - Trademarks
    - Patents
    - Copyrights
    - Licenses and licensing agreements
6. Material assets
    - Inventory
    - Property, plant and equipment (PP&E)
    - Real estate
    - Technology
7. Contracts
    - Customer and supplier contracts
    - Guarantees, loans and credit agreements
    - Agreements of partnership or joint venture
    - Franchising agreements
    - Employment contracts
8. Employees and management
9. Litigation
    - Outstanding legal liabilities (pending or threatened)
10. Regulatory and compliance matters
    - Any outstanding regulatory issues for the target company
    - Potential regulatory issues with the proposed transaction (namely, antitrust)

If all goes well, a legally binding purchase and sale contract is agreed, the financing is finalised and the deal is closed. Once the deal is finalised, while the transaction may be completed, it is only really the end of the beginning for management, as the key work of integration begins. This can be a substantial undertaking, requiring months if not years. In addition to the synergies identified, roles and responsibilities, structure, finances and remuneration structures likely all need adjusting.

Not all negotiations are as amicable of course, and it can be the case that neither the board nor management agree to the takeover. Multi-billion-dollar examples include when Kraft announced its intention to acquire Cadbury, the RBS acquisition of ABN Amro and the Sanofi-Aventis acquisition of Genzyme. Beyond offering a higher price, in these instances if the acquirer wants to still go ahead, it is known as a hostile takeover, and rather than communicating with management, the acquirer will go direct to shareholders. There are two key tools then at the acquirer's disposal: a tender offer and a proxy fight. A tender offer is achieved by the acquirer making an offer to shareholders to sell their shares – almost always at a reasonable premium. A proxy fight is more complex and involves the acquirer convincing other shareholders to vote in its favour and force out senior management to make it easier for control to be taken of the organisation. Out of the two, a simple tender offer to shareholders will normally be preferable to the acquirer.

There are of course methods for management to fight against a hostile takeover. These include, for example, having stocks with different voting rights. For example, Mark Zuckerberg does not have a majority holding in Facebook, but he has dictatorial powers over voting because the majority of shares that he does own have ten times the voting power of the shares publicly traded on the exchange. Other mechanisms include 'golden parachute' contracts for management which guarantee substantial payoffs in the event of a hostile takeover, and 'poison pill' plans that grant existing shareholders the right to purchase additional shares at a discount, diluting the interest of any hostile party. All these hostile takeover schemes are nearly always shareholder unfriendly, and therefore some are outlawed in certain geographies.

Developing a merger model

A merger model reflects the combined post-deal financial outlook of the acquiring company and the acquired. As it is forward looking and can be supplied to shareholders, the financial statements from such a model must be referred to as 'pro forma' financial statements. This reflects that these post-deal estimates are very preliminary in nature.

At the most basic level, an M&A model simply combines the financial statements of two companies. However, one plus one very rarely equals two when it comes to these transactions. Synergies need to be recognised, deal financing structure accounted for, and elements like goodwill and asset value adjustments made. In total, the process can be broken down into four key steps:

1. Model the outlook of each company individually
2. Develop deal assumptions and supporting schedules
3. Create a closing balance sheet
4. Develop the pro forma financial statements.

You will note that the first and final stages both use the project and value framework detailed earlier. The only real difference, therefore, is the middle stage. For this stage, we will need to create deal assumptions, develop supporting deal schedules and build a closing balance sheet.

In terms of formatting, much like a simple company projection, colours should be used to separate hard coded cells and assumptions to avoid error. Best practice is to have a separate tab for each of the two companies being modelled, one for deal assumptions, and then a final pro forma tab that details the pro forma financial statements plus valuation output of the combined company.

Deal assumptions

The assumptions for an M&A model can be split into transaction, financing and synergy assumptions. Financing assumptions will affect largely the balance sheet, while synergy assumptions focus only on the income statement impact. As a company will not have historical figures for many of these assumptions, some guidance has been provided below on common ranges for these items.

Transaction		
	Target price	Current price
	Takeover premium (%)	Often 15% to 25%
	Cash consideration (%)	0% to 100%
	Share discount (%)	Often 3-6%
Financing		
	Debt funding ($)	Based on capital structure
	Equity issuance fees (%)	Typically c.3%
	Debt issuance fees (%)	Typically c.3%
	Debt interest rate (%)	Look at market rates
	Other closing costs ($)	Largely professional fees
Synergies		
	Revenue enhancement (% or $)	% of Sales or $ amount
	COGS* savings (% or $)	% of Costs or $ amount
	OPEX** savings (% or $)	% of OPEX or $ amount
	Synergies realised in Year 1 (full year)	0%-100%
	Synergies realised in Year 2	0%-100%
	Synergies Realised in Year 3+	100%

**COGS: cost of goods sold*

***OPEX: operational expenses (in practice, best broken down line by line)*

Transaction assumptions

Transaction assumptions include the takeover premium, cash consideration and share issuance discount. These are all percentage figures and can vary based on the companies involved and the broader market backdrop. For example, the takeover premium during a period of market weakness is likely to be lower than in an otherwise rising market, ranging typically from 15% to 25%. So, if the company was listed and trading at $10 per share and the assumed takeover premium was 20%, then the actual purchase price would be $12 ($10 × 120% = $12).

The cash consideration assumption is the portion of the merger or acquisition that is not funded by an equity issuance. This can range from 0% to 100% and, while this balance does not receive the attention of the purchase price, it is a critical part in determining the ultimate return and risk profile of the deal. In the instance that stock is selected as the currency of choice for the transaction, the risk that the synergies are not realised is shared between both the acquirer and the target, while in a cash transaction all the deal economics are the acquirer's.

Studies have shown that at the time of announcement, shareholders in the acquiring company do better in cash transactions than in stock transactions. What's more, these performance differences become greater over time. This is probably because if the acquirer believes that its own share price is undervalued and is confident about deal synergies, then a clear-cut cash transaction is preferable. Despite this, since the 1980s, one of the big shifts in M&A has been the rise of deals paid for in stock, and it is now not unusual for 30% to 50% of deals to have a stock component.

The share issuance discount is only applicable if there is a stock consideration element to the deal. This is the discount (if any) applied to the current market price to determine the number of shares that the target receives. It is typically required, especially for listed firms, to make holding the shares an attractive option for the target's investors. The extent of any discount will depend on market conditions and how well the deal is received. The acquirer will want to give as limited a discount as possible, often ranging from 2% to 5%. This makes clear communicating and marketing of the advantages of the deal to shareholders an important step of any equity issuance plans, in order that the discount can be reduced and consequently fewer additional shares issued.

Financing assumptions

The extent to which financing assumptions are required will largely depend on the financing structure chosen for the deal. For instance, if it is a merger, or the acquisition requires no equity or debt financing, then only professional fees may be required. These might include fees to consultants, lawyers or accountants.

If external funding is sought from a debt or equity issuance beyond the amount raised, issuance fees must also be accounted for. These refer to the amount that the investment bank receives for organising the deal and are calculated as a percentage of the amount raised. This is similar to how an estate agent takes his or her fee as a percentage of the house price when sold. In the case of investment banks, the fee is normally around 3%, although this can vary based on the size of the deal and the level of confidence that there will be investor appetite. A larger issuance size or a deal for which there is likely high demand may achieve a lower fee. Conversely, a lower issuance size or a deal for which there is less investor appetite may require a higher fee. For debt, an 'underwritten' deal is when the bank first buys the shares or debt and then sells to investors, thereby guaranteeing issuance success for the company at an early stage.

Synergy assumptions

Finally, synergy assumptions are required. These involve the most subjective assumptions, as there will be no historical precedent and every deal will be unique in terms of what benefits it can bring to the table. The deal assumptions will likely be highly dependent on the acquirer. Ultimately, the more value an acquirer stands to create from the combined entity, the more it can justify paying for the firm and therefore outbid competition.

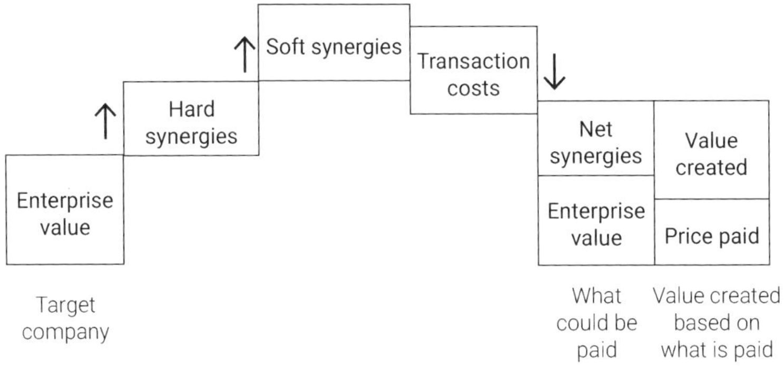

Synergies are typically split between hard synergies and soft synergies. Hard synergies are direct, easily identifiable cost synergies. In terms of costs that directly affect the cost of goods sold (COGS), these can include lower unit production costs due to greater scale benefits, shared technology platforms or supply chain efficiencies. Operational expenditure (OPEX) hard synergies can be even more evident – for instance, reduced management headcount, efficiencies in sales and marketing, research and development. In the assumptions section of our M&A model, these synergies will require quantifying, and an assessment will need to be made over what period they can be fully realised. This is known as the phase-in period.

Soft synergies are more difficult to model with accuracy as they are less identifiable. They arise from incremental revenue beyond the combined entity. The most common soft synergy is access to new customers for existing products. This might include different distribution channels in a local market or an entirely different geographical reach. For example, if a UK company merged with a Chinese one, and up until the deal it had been focused only on its domestic markets, post-deal it would likely look for ways it could use the new relationship to expand its product reach beyond its core market. Another frequent example of a soft synergy is intellectual property or patents. These can help make the products of the combined entity more competitive, and therefore lift revenue as consumer demand rises.

In the case of both hard and soft synergies, a phase-in period will likely be needed to recognise the time required to realise change. Hence, the actual synergy in any given period will be equal to the value of the synergy assumption multiplied by the percent realised in that period assumption. For example, if the revenue enhancement was calculated to be $1 million, and in Year 1 the amount realised was assumed to be 20%, that would be equal to $200,000 of additional revenue in that year (20% × $1 million = $200,000). In the second year after deal completion, if 40% of deal synergies were assumed to be completed, that additional revenue would rise to $400,000 (40% × $1 million = $400,000), and so on. In the case of revenue enhancement, in each year this is added to the combined revenue of the two entities. In the case that the synergy is a cost synergy, such as COGS or OPEX, it is a saving and should be subtracted from the cost of the combined entities.

Outside of synergies, there can be a range of other reasons for M&A, such as business diversification, tax benefits, gaining access to unique capabilities and unlocking hidden value.

While deals can create considerable benefits, there are also M&A risks. Integration can often prove harder in practice than in theory. Indeed, studies have demonstrated that for publicly listed companies, the acquirer's share price in most cases underperforms in the years subsequent to a deal. The reasons for this vary, but can include cultural clashes between companies (often the case when a high-growth company purchases a low-growth one), overpayment due to overly ambitious forward projections of the acquired company, and integration risk (inability to realise the forecast synergies).

Deal supporting schedules

With assumptions developed, the next step is to create deal supporting schedules. As per the supporting schedules for a company's financial projections, these are simply a means of laying out calculations to avoid error, while ensuring that our working is clear and can be easily followed. These are best placed on the deal assumption tab, to ensure that cell references are easy to track. There are four key deal supporting schedules: balance sheet cash, goodwill allocation, integration, and pro forma shares outstanding.

Closing balance sheet cash

The closing balance sheet reflects the balance sheet of the merged entity upon completion, and will therefore also equal the opening balance sheet value when forecasting for line items such as cash, debt and PP&E. The closing balance sheet cash amount includes not just the combined cash balances, but also all the financing cash flows and fees.

Cash balance company A	Input from balance sheet
Cash balance company B	Input from balance sheet
Cash consideration	−(Purchase price × cash consideration % (a))
Debt issued	Debt issuance (a)
Debt financing fees	−(Debt replacement × Debt financing fee % (a))
Equity financing fees	−(Stock consideration* × Equity financing fee % (a))
Other fees	−(Other closing costs (a))
Cash required	Sum all the above

**Stock consideration = Purchase price × (1 − Cash consideration)*

Notably, the stock consideration is not a part of this supporting schedule, as it represents a non-cash payment (shares are issued in lieu of cash).

Goodwill

Once completed, the goodwill allocation schedule needs developing. This is required as most acquisitions are done at a price in excess of book value. Therefore, to reflect the total deal value on the balance sheet, the target company value must be broken down between recognised accounting assets and 'goodwill'.

Goodwill = Purchase price – Adjusted book value

So, if a company had a book value of $5 million and was purchased for $7 million, the $5 million of book value would be combined with the acquirer's assets and then $2 million ($7 million – $5 million = $2 million) recognised on the acquirer's balance sheet as 'goodwill'. The acquiring company is however allowed to revalue the target's assets to 'fair value' post deal. However, changes are not normally substantial and typically only affect property, plant and equipment (PPE), inventory, and identifiable intangible assets such as patents.

While the name 'goodwill' suggests that a premium is paid out of generosity, what it actually reflects is the value of non-identifiable intangible assets, such as brand name, technology developed within the firm and customer base. As noted in accounting, management will often want to understate the fair value of assets so that more is allocated to goodwill. This is because goodwill is not amortised or depreciated over time and therefore this raises company accrual profits, thereby making the deal look particularly attractive. While this may reflect favourably on management, it actually harms the underlying value of the company, as higher profits mean higher taxes and therefore lower actual cash flows.

Integration

The integration supporting schedule develops the inputs for the pro forma sales to operating profit line of the income statement projections. Each line includes the combined projected figures of each entity, plus or minus the synergy assumption. To develop it, the first step is to add together the individual line items for both companies – namely, sales, cost of goods sold (COGS) and individual operational expenditure items such as marketing, research, etc.

The second step is to create a line to adjust for the synergy assumptions. In each case, the synergy adjustment in a given year will be equal to the value of the adjustment multiplied by the percentage synergy realised in that year. In the case the synergy enhancement/saving is a percentage rather than a currency value, it will require being multiplied against the relevant income statement line first. So for example, in the case that COGS savings were assumed to be 5% and combined COGS were $100 million, that would equal a COGS saving value of $5 million ($100 million × 5% = $5 million). Once 100% of synergies have been achieved, it is assumed that all these synergies will carry forward in future periods.

	Input year
Revenue (Company A)	Input from income statement
Revenue (Company B)	Input from income statement
Synergies	Sales enhancement (a) × Synergy realised (a)
Total	A Revenue + B Revenue + Synergies

	Input year
COGS (Company A)	COGS from income statement
COGS (Company B)	COGS from income statement
Synergies	COGS saving (a) × Synergy realised (a)
Total	A COGS + B COGS – Synergies

	Input year
OPEX (Company A)	OPEX from income statement
OPEX (Company B)	OPEX from income statement
Synergies	OPEX saving (a) × Synergy realised (a)
Total	A OPEX + B OPEX – Synergies

(a) = assumption

This will provide the inputs for the pro forma income statement sales down to operating expenses.

Shares outstanding

Making a company larger is easy – adding per share value, less so. It is therefore important to measure success or failure in terms of the deal's impact on the share value, and to do this, the post-deal number of shares must be accounted for. In the event that there is no stock consideration, the number of shares pre- and post-deal will be exactly the same. If, however, stock is used as a means of transaction currency, then the overall number of shares will rise by the number of shares issued to the target company's shareholders.

Stock consideration	Equity valuation × (1 – Cash consideration (a))
Share issue price	Acquirer share price × (1 – Share discount (a))
Shares issued	Stock consideration* ÷ Share issue price
Pro forma shares outstanding	Acquirer's shares + Shares issued

**Stock consideration = Purchase price × (1 - Cash consideration)*

The pro forma outstanding share figure will be used when calculating for the per share value of the company. For the purpose of calculating how much each share of the target company will receive, the share exchange ratio can also be calculated. This is simply the offer price divided by the acquirer's share price.

$$\text{Share exchange ratio} = \frac{\text{Offer price}}{\text{Acquirer's share price}}$$

For example, if (including the takeover premium) the offer price was $10 per share and the share price of the acquiring company was $5, then the acquirer would need to issue 2 of its own shares for every 1 share of the Target it seeks to acquire ($10 ÷ $5 =2). This would be in addition to any cash component that the deal was structured to also pay out to target holders.

Closing balance sheet

Finally, a closing balance sheet is developed to reflect the deal impact. As always, it is essential that the balance sheet balances – that is, debt plus equity is equal to assets. The below balance sheet outlines how key line items are amended.

Cash	Cash change (ss)
Receivables	Combine
Inventory	Combine (adjusted to fair value if changes made)
PP&E	Combine (adjusted to fair value if changes made)
Goodwill	Combine + Goodwill (ss)
Assets	Sum asset items
Payables	Combined
Debt	Combine + Debt raised (ss) – Debt financing fee (ss)
Liabilities	Sum liability items
Equity capital	Acquirer's equity capital + Add stock issued (ss)
Retained earnings	Acquirer's retained earnings – Fees (ss)
Equity	Sum equity items

(ss) = supporting schedule

The big-picture changes that are made to the balance sheet include that assets and liabilities are combined and that equity increases by an amount equal to the stock issued. The smaller changes are then reflecting fair value adjustments, fees and others.

Pro forma model

With all the groundwork now completed, the pro forma financial statements can finally be developed. This is done using the exact steps previously outlined in the chapter titled projecting returns. The only difference is that from sales to operating profit, the inputs are derived from the deal supporting schedule, as opposed to connecting to operating activity assumptions. This means that some of the 'assumptions' will be 'not needed'.

Income statement	
Sales growth	Not needed
Gross margin	Not needed
Distribution expense (percent of sales)	Not needed
Marketing & admin expense (fixed cost)	Not needed
Research expense (percent of sales)	Not needed
Depreciation (percent of sales)	% of sales
Long-term debt interest expense	% of total long-term average debt
Tax rate (percent of EBT)	% of EBIT

Balance sheet	
Capital asset turnover ratio	Sales ÷ Average PPE
Receivable days (sales basis)	(Receivables ÷ Sales) × 365
Inventory days (COGS basis)	(Inventory ÷ Costs) × 365
Payable days (COGS basis)	(Payables ÷ Costs) × 365
Income tax payable	% of tax expense
Long-term debt	Local currency amount outstanding
Common share capital	Local currency amount outstanding
Dividend payout ratio	% of Profit

In a number of instances, there will be a greater degree of subjectivity, as there is no historical legacy of a post-deal company to draw upon. If one company is substantially larger than the other, this will not necessarily cause problems, as the past experience of the larger company can be heavily leaned on and then marginally adjusted for the smaller company. However, if the companies are a similar size in most respects, some form of weighted average across the two companies should be used.

As per the prior steps to create a financial model, once the assumptions are developed, then carry out the creation of the supporting schedules for working capital, depreciation and debt. Then use these to help complete the balance sheet and income statement. Finally, use assumptions and changes in the balance sheet between periods to complete the cash flow statement. Ultimately, as always, the key measure of whether the inputs have been correctly formulated will be if the balance sheet balances.

With regards to valuation, the steps are then exactly the same. However, when considering the multiple or discount rate, ensure that it is the post-deal risk and return outlook that is being reflected, not the former profile of the company (as with the assumptions, this may require some subjective adjustment to historical norms). Finally, do not forget to use the pro forma outstanding shares when calculating for per share value.

Deal analysis

The primary means of evaluating the deal will be to assess how much per share value the deal adds. In the event that the deal is accretive, an offer will likely be put forward. In the event that the post-deal valuation would be lower, it should be rejected. In practice, there will be far more nuance to the decision process, as multiple options are typically weighed and resources are limited. Therefore, opportunities are normally ranked in order of attractiveness.

Beyond a deal's impact on a company's intrinsic valuation, its impact on the credit statistics and financial ratios should also be monitored. This should include the deal's impact on earnings per share. Will it be accretive? And if so, when? This is an important measure, as many investors use relative valuation to value a company, and therefore the earnings per share impact will be the key variable that drives their valuation.

Summary

Developing an M&A financial model is considerably more time-consuming than creating one for a single company. However, while additional assumptions are required, there is little further actual complexity. It comes down to an adjusted combination of two companies to formulate the financial statements, after which the actual resulting valuation stage remains the same.

Leveraged Buyouts

"Leverage: don't make deals without it.
Enhance" – Donald J. Trump

Acquisitions, like companies, can involve financial leverage. In the case of a strategic acquisition by a company, the focus is largely on the operational efficiencies that can be found. For a financial buyer, however, there are often no operational synergies to be gained, and therefore the deal comes down to financial efficiencies – namely, leverage. Applying leverage involves the use of considerable debt funding to finance a transaction, which in turn can amplify any gains. This can transform even the most mundane of purchases into a high-risk venture with considerable potential upside for equity investors. These deals are known as leveraged buyouts.

Due to the high-risk nature of a heavily leveraged balance sheet, leveraged buyers are largely limited to low-risk companies – firms with predictable outlooks and reasonable collateral. However, during times of easy credit and strong risk appetite, standards often drop. Prior to the 2008 financial crisis, it was not uncommon for debt funding to account for over 90% of an LBO deal's financing, but in more recent years, use of debt funding is far more 'restrained', accounting for 50% to 70%. While this makes LBOs lower risk than in the past, it is still a form of highly geared investment, and therefore needs further consideration when being valued.

The primary actor in an LBO is nearly always a private equity fund. These pool capital to make long-term investment in private companies or take a public company private. Some of the larger private equity companies in this space include Blackstone, Neuberger Berman, Apollo, KKR and Carlyle. Private equity funds became popular following the rampant empire building of many companies in the 1960s. Poor governance and bloated layers of middle management reduced efficiencies, creating unnecessary cost pressures and poor capital allocation. The environment was ripe for equity funds to come in and shake up these companies. Often, this involved selling large chunks of the business to better realise value – a process that led to them being often labelled 'corporate raiders'.

Nowadays, while there are still 'buy and build' styled transactions, where synergies are forced through the target, many LBOs are simply highly geared buy and hold investments. One of the larger LBOs in recent history involved the purchase of Hilton Hotels by Blackstone for just over $20 billion in 2007. Despite the transaction being completed right at the height of the market, just prior to the global financial crisis, Blackstone's exit in 2018 netted a profit of $14 billion. Other large-scale LBOs have included AB Alliance's acquisition of Boots for $19.6 billion in 2014, the $21 billion LBO of Heathrow airport in 2006, and the LBO of Heinz in 2013. While the gains from these deals can be exceptional, history is also littered with the stories of LBOs gone wrong. Energy Future Holdings remains still the largest LBO target in history, valued at over $30 billion when purchased in an LBO transaction in 2007. Within seven years however, it had defaulted on $35.8 billion of loans and bonds, wiping out the firm's entire equity value – a valuable reminder of the risk that comes with extensive leverage.

Developing detailed debt assumptions

Fortunately, an LBO model is exactly the same as any other M&A model in nearly every aspect. There are two differences, however. The first is that often no synergy assumptions are required, as the purpose for buying is often purely financial rather than strategic. The second difference is that due to the extent that leverage influences the return outcome, greater detailing within the debt assumptions is prudent to ensure that company cash flows can meet debt payments.

In the company financial model and M&A pro forma model, the two assumptions driving debt projections were simply a headline outstanding debt figure and an interest rate assumption. For an LBO model however, each tranche of debt is individually broken out, the outstanding debt balance is calculated as a multiple of EBITDA (debt multiple or 'DM'), and the amortisation schedule is listed. Below is an example of what that might look like.

Financing sources

Type	Debt Multiple (DM)	Value	Financing fee	Interest rate
Cash		Balance sheet cash		-
Term loan 1	2.5	EBITDA × DM	1.5%	5%
Term loan	2x	EBITDA × DM	1.5%	6%
Subordinated debt	1.5	EBITDA × DM	1.5%	8%
Sponsors' equity	-	Invested cash		-

Loan amortisation schedule

	Year 1	Year 2	Year 3	Year 4	Year 5
Term loan 1	20%	20%	20%	20%	20%
Term loan 2	10%	10%	80%		
Subordinated debt					100%

Further details on debt financing assumptions are provided below.

Debt to EBITDA multiple

Debt borrowing is not infinite. Just like the bank may limit how much it lends you for a mortgage to purchase a house, so too will it limit how much debt it extends to a private equity company in a deal. As noted previously, net debt to equity is a helpful calculation in terms of capital structure, but debt to EBITDA is a more appropriate measure when considering debt payment affordability. For this reason, LBO deals are typically framed in terms of how many multiples of EBITDA can be raised. The exact amount varies between periods, although it is typically 3x to 6x the target company's EBITDA over the past 12 months. So for example, if in the prior 12 months before a deal the target company had produced $100 million of EBITDA, and the bank was willing to lend 3x EBITDA, that would be equal to $300 million of debt.

Cash flow structure

Debt is a broad term for a variety of structures with different terms and repayment schedules. An important concept here is the capital stack – who has rights to the company's earnings before interest and tax, and in what order. As we know, equity holders come last, but even across the debt holders there is an order of priority. In the event of liquidation, for example, this will determine who has first dibs on the company assets and who has to wait in line. In the event that all cash debt payments cannot be made, it will determine who takes priority.

The key difference in this respect is between secured lenders – which have a direct claim on certain assets – and unsecured lenders, which rank second. Say, for instance, you financed the purchase of a car with both bank borrowing and credit card borrowing. The bank would almost certainly require the car as collateral and would therefore be considered a secure lender that could make a claim on the car in the event of default. The credit card lender meanwhile would provide money on easier terms and would have no claim to the vehicle if repayments were not made. Suffice to say, due to the different risk levels between the bank loan (secured) and credit card debt (unsecured), the rate on the bank borrowing would be far lower than that on the credit card. So too with LBO debt funding. As a consequence, bank debt is preferable and lower cost, but it can be supplemented with higher-cost unsecured lending if the rate on that borrowing is still below the cost of equity.

In the cases of both secured and unsecured debt, an amortisation schedule must be developed for each tranche. This breaks down what percentage of total mandatory principal must be repaid each year, and therefore should sum to 100% (full repayment by the end). The structure of these payments is commonly either equal annual repayments, or simply one repayment in the final year. The amortisation schedule is required to ensure that required cash principal repayments can be met – something that is not obvious in the income statement due to the capitalisation of debt creating possible differences between cash payments and income statement recognition.

DEVELOPING A DEBT SCHEDULE FOR THE PRO FORMA FINANCIAL STATEMENTS

The debt schedule for an LBO is broken down by issuance, with each issuance independently modelled. For the balance sheet, as usual, the year-end closing balance is equal to the opening balance minus any repayments. However, for an LBO model, the repayment value is equal to the original acquisition debt balance multiplied by the period debt schedule assumption. For example, if $10 million of debt had been issued to fund the deal, and in Year 3 an assumption that 30% would be repaid had been inputted, then the value in that year for repayment would be $30 million ($100 million × 30% = $30 million).

Opening balance	Prior-year closing balance
Repayment	Acquisition debt (a) × Period debt schedule (a)
Closing balance	Opening balance – Repayments

As with the balance sheet debt, the interest expense for each tranche is also independently calculated. This is done as per any other financial model – by taking the average of the current-year and prior-year balances, then multiplying by the interest rate assumption.

Interest expense = Interest rate (a) × Average debt balance

As every tranche has been modelled independently, the final step for the schedule is to sum up each tranche to develop a single closing balance and single interest expense figure. These will be used as the inputs for the pro forma balance sheet and income statement.

Deal analysis

In the case of M&A, the end company is assumed to have an infinite life and the attractiveness of the deal is therefore primarily based on how accretive it is to the company's NAV. For a leveraged buyout, however, because in most cases it is assumed that the company will be exited, it has a finite life and we can measure its appeal based on the return from acquisition to exit. This is done by calculating for the internal rate of return (IRR). The IRR is the compound annual rate of return and is equal to the required return that when used as the discount rate makes all cash flows equal to zero.

$$\text{PV} = \sum \frac{\text{Cash flows}}{(1 + \text{IRR})}$$

The IRR is an insightful means of measuring returns, as it does not just take into account the magnitude of returns, but also the timing of cash flows. While you could derive it through trial and error, fortunately it is easy to calculate on Excel by inputting '=IRR', followed by the bracketed annual cash flows. In the example below, this would be equal to '=IRR(B2:E2)' and the outcome would equal 26%. If this 26% were then inputted as the required return for cash flows (in this case a single cash flow in Year 3) and the initial current-year investment deducted, then if your inputs have been correct this will equal 0.

	A	B	C	D	E
1		2021	2022	2023	2024
2	Cash flow	-\$10,000	0	0	\$20,000

$$\$0 = \frac{\$20{,}000}{(1 + 0.26)^3} - \$10{,}000$$

The cash flow normally used for the purpose of the IRR calculation is the cash flow to equity holders. This is the tangible return to shareholders and is therefore most immediately relevant in terms of what an investor will make. For analytical purposes, however, the 'unlevered IRR' should also be calculated using cash flow to the firm, to measure performance irrespective of capital structure. As long as the IRR is positive, this will be a lower figure, and in the event that the unlevered returns are negligible, serious questions should be asked about whether the deal is worth pursuing at all. Bear in mind that the targeted levered IRR for an LBO is typically 20% to 30%. However, due to the financial risks of that investment, the required return will also be high to compensate the investor for that risk.

While IRR is important, it is not the only factor to be considered. A company may rank investment opportunities according to their IRR, but ultimately the dollar return will also play a sizeable part in the decision process. To take an extreme example, if you ran a $1 billion private equity fund and you had to make a choice between a 100% return for an investment in a company where the dollar return on capital was $1 million and a company with an IRR of 40% but a return of $100 million, you would almost certainly select the latter. Scale does therefore matter, and should be a part of the deal consideration process.

One final consideration with regards to deal analysis is how confident the acquirer will be in achieving the exit multiple projected. Typically, private equity funds have a finite life of around ten years, and within this the holding period is only normally around six years. Therefore, a realistic exit strategy needs to be developed if the values projected are to be realised.

There are several forms an exit could take. These include a secondary sale to another private equity fund, a sale to a strategic buyer, or even a management buyout. Typically, a strategic buyer is preferred, as in this case the purchaser can realise synergies and therefore justify paying a higher price upon purchase. A further option for larger-sized LBOs is a public listing via an initial public offering (IPO). The benefit of listing the business is that the company will have access to large amounts of capital and, due to the increase in share trading liquidity, the valuation will not suffer from the marketability discount that can hamper private market valuations. The disadvantage to an IPO is that it is a costly and time-consuming process. In addition, while shares can be sold during the IPO, public equity investors will normally still be keen to see that the private equity firm does not exit entirely and therefore a full exit will only be achievable over the subsequent months or years.

Summary

The emphasis of an LBO model relative to a M&A model is shifted from detailed operational synergy assumptions to far more detailed assumptions driving the pro forma debt and interest outputs. These are highly leveraged transactions, meaning particular care must be taken when analysing the risk and return profile of the deal, as outcomes tend to be far more black and white than in a traditional M&A. Finally, the IRR as a measure of return is an industry standard and must be understood in order to properly assess the attractiveness of a deal.

Start-ups & Early-stage Companies

'A big business starts small' – Richard Branson

All companies start small. Be it Microsoft in Bill Gates's garage or Facebook in the student halls of Harvard, the early years of a company's development are exciting but often unglamorous and filled with uncertainty. For the financial analyst, there is little information that you can really get your teeth into and draw solid conclusions from, and a very real risk that the company will not survive beyond a few years. With sizeable risks however come sizeable gains, and while a start-up may only have a one-in-ten chance of ever making money for shareholders, when that does happen, the returns can be phenomenal.

Venture capital investing

Financing for early-stage companies is normally initially derived from family, friends and personal savings, but for a company to make a meaningful acceleration forward it will likely quickly require larger-scale institutional capital. This is normally derived from venture capital (VC) funds. Venture capital provides finance and operational expertise for entrepreneurs and start-up companies. From Google to Facebook, many of the world's large technology companies can trace their financial origins back to VC funding. These funds typically focus on sectors such as technology, healthcare, cleantech, biotech or fintech, and can take a company from often little more than an idea to a far more tangible business with sales, an established team and a path to profitability.

There are a number of key distinctions between traditional private equity buyout funds, such as the leveraged buyout funds described in the last chapter, and VC. The first and most notable is the type of target company profile. A buyout fund will typically focus on companies with steady and predictable cash flows, an experienced management team, a strong market position, established products and a potential for cost reduction or restructuring. Venture capital target companies often have low cash flow predictability, a lack of market history, a newly formed management team, greater uncertainty over the exit route, and in the near term they probably have a high cash burn rate.

For an early-stage company, financing is typically split into rounds rather than a single large capital raise. The key stages are pre-seed financing, seed financing, then series A, B, C and sometimes even D financing.

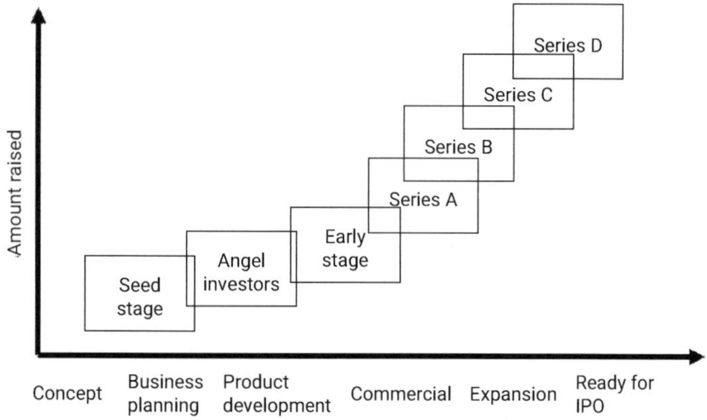

Pre-seed funding is the earliest stage. The most common participants are the founder and his or her family and friends. This is really just to get operations off the ground and is often largely dominated by the resources of the founder/founders. The seed stage is then the first really official stage of funding. Venture capital might get involved at this stage, but it is most common for angel investors to participate. Angel investors are typically high net worth individuals seeking high-risk, high-return opportunities, although the advent of online crowdfunding platforms has made angel investing far more accessible to less-well-off investors looking to invest only a small amount at a time. The seed funding step can help a company conduct market research and product development. While the amount can vary dramatically based on geography, sector and time, companies looking for seed funding typically raise between $10,000 and $2 million and are usually valued at between $3 million and $6 million.

Once a company has developed a product and is producing revenue, series A funding is the next fundraising stage. This round is dominated by venture capital investors, providing funding normally to optimise the product and scale it across different markets. At this point, the company will need a proper strategy and roadmap on how it is going to reach profitability. A typical series A round may raise $2 million to $15 million and be done at a valuation of around $20 million. It will often be led by a few investors or a single lead investor, who will then attract additional syndicate investors to the deal. Angel investors may also participate, but by this stage their participation is more marginal than at the seed stage.

If further funding is still required, series B funding can then be raised. This often involves the same set of investors that invested at the series A round, and the capital raised is used to really take the business to the next level. A company at this point would have demonstrated success, have a large user base and be seeking to scale up. This may, for instance, require greater spending on business development, advertising and overall support. The company's valuation at this point would have likely reached around $30 million to $60 million, and the amount raised would likely be around $30 million.

If a business makes it to series C funding, then it is likely already prospering. Its purpose for raising capital might include developing new products, entering new markets or even acquisition. At this point, the company would have almost certainly outgrown venture capital funding and be seeking finance from private equity funds, with the help of investment banks. Some companies also progress on to a series D funding if the goals set out in the series C round have not been achieved and they are keen to publicly list.

Valuation

The principal steps for valuing a start-up are the same as those taken to value a more mature company. It can be valued relative to other companies or valued based on its cash flows. There are however differences that need addressing, as often there are no financial data points to anchor a relative valuation to, and cash flows to create a discounted cash flow model are likely to be even further afield. The below methods are therefore adapted to take account of this. And while they are no doubt clunky, both are a robust means of deriving an estimated value.

Relative valuation

The most common relative valuation approach is the development stage methodology. This uses the typical valuation ranges at which transactions have taken place, to then determine what may be a fair value for the subject company being assessed. It is the most basic form of relative valuation, requires no company financials, is grounded in recent market transactions, and is broadly understood by both entrepreneurs and investors. The below is an example of some basic valuation ranges for a start-up company.

Company value	Stage
$250,000 – $500,000	Has an exciting idea or business plan
$500,000 – $1 million	Strong management team in place to execute on the plan
$1 million – $2 million	Has a final product/prototype
$2 million – $5 million	Has signs of a customer base (commitments/partners)
>$5 million	Achieving revenue and has a path to profitability

While this method is convenient, simple and quick, bear in mind that these ranges are dynamic across time and fluctuate with the market cycle, dropping in a recession and rising during periods of strong economic expansion.

Beyond market volatility, the end valuation for a company will also be heavily influenced by its specific attributes. For instance, you would likely adjust the price up if it was Elon Musk pitching an idea, but down if it was a first-time entrepreneur with a limited track record in his or her field.

While rough judgements are often made from experience and intuition, there are ways to refine the process so that it is more methodical. One way to do this is to use the scorecard approach. Using 100% as the baseline, this adjusts a company's value relative to a peer group of comparative transactions, based on a number of factors that are considered predictive of future success. These factors typically pertain to people, markets, products (or technology), marketing and financing needs. Summing to 100%, a weight is attached to each factor, based on how important it is within the scorecard – the higher the weight, the more it will influence the end output. These weights will often vary between investors based on their own interpretation of what will drive value creation. An example scorecard is however illustrated below.

Factor	Characteristics to look for	Weight
People	Track record, experience, chance that the right people will be available to drive company growth	35%
Market	Value of the addressable market, competitive intensity, growth prospects	15%
Product	Features, trials, testing, competitiveness	25%
Marketing	The ease with which the product can be brought to market, any existing or likely partnership opportunities	10%
Funding needs	The likelihood and extent to which the company will require additional capital	10%
Others	Anything else that may affect value relative to comparable	5%
Sum		100%

Once weights have been inputted, the next step is to create a confidence factor for each line, using 100% as the base rate to reflect an inline score. Areas of relative weakness will score below 100%, while relative strengths will be scored above 100%. Bear in mind that scores are relative to the companies used in the valuation peer group, and not a reflection of absolute attractiveness. For example, a company may have a strong team of individuals running it, but if those individuals are not quite as competent as those at the peer companies used for comparison, it would receive a score below 100%.

Once weights have been developed and confidence factors estimated, the two are multiplied along each row to produce a weighted factor.

These weighted factors, when summed together, will then equal the scorecard 'score'. In the example below, the score would be 110%.

Factor	Weight	Confidence factor	Weighted factor
People	35%	120%	42%
Market	15%	80%	12%
Product/technology	25%	130%	33%
Marketing/sales/ partnership	10%	90%	9%
Further investment	10%	90%	9%
Others	5%	110%	5.5%
Sum			110%

This score is then multiplied by the peer average to arrive at an adjusted value. For example, if the peer average valuation was $2 million, and if you determined that the total scorecard score was 110%, then the adjusted value would be $2.2 million – calculated as $2 million x 110% = $2.2 million.

Intrinsic value

The 'venture capital method' is the primary means of intrinsic valuation for early-stage or start-up companies. Just like the method for more mature companies, it is based on discounting cash flows. However, instead of valuing the company based on its total discounted cash flows to the firm or equity, only the investor's direct return is captured in the venture capital method. That is, how much is invested, and how much is received upon exit.

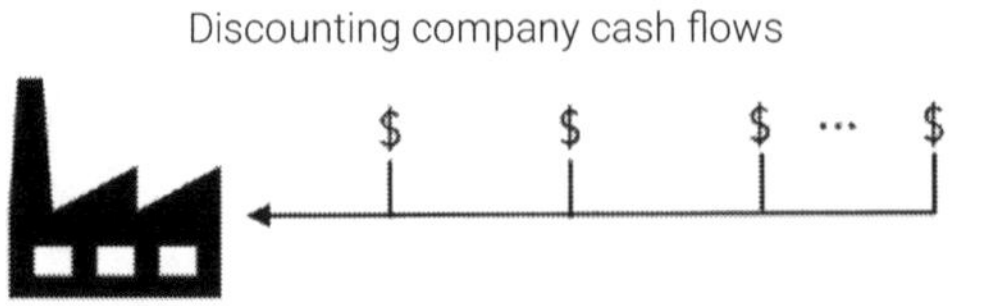

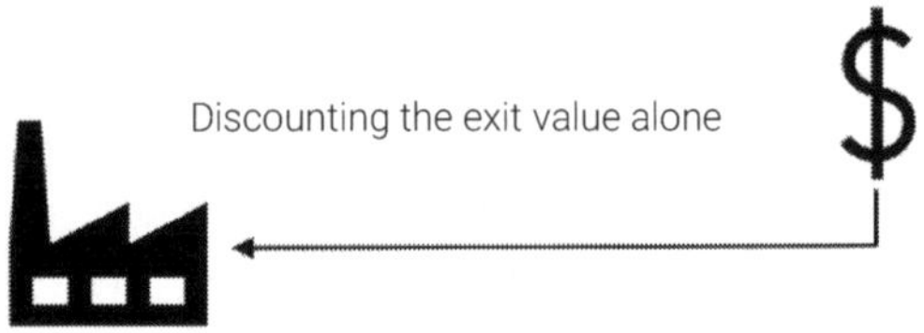

Unlike valuing a more mature company, the purpose of valuation for an early-stage company is almost always to participate in a financing round, rather than to simply transact in shares. As a result, it is not as simple as determining a present value and dividing that by the number of shares for the price, as new shares issued in exchange for the investment must also be accounted for. It is therefore a three-step process:

1. Determine the exit value
2. Discount that to a present value
3. Calculate the percentage of the company required for an investment, and use this to calculate for the post-deal number of shares.

Stage 1 – determine a terminal value

The first step is determining a future value for the company – the value that an investor would expect to get at exit. With the passing of time, the company will develop and its outlook become far more assured. At this point, a future value will be far more concrete than a present one. For example, an investor would have been far more confident in the prospects of Facebook when it was in Year 5 or 6 of operations than when it was little more than a business plan concocted in a dormitory at Harvard University. The more a company matures, the less the uncertainty, and consequently the more stable the valuation.

There is no hard rule with regards to how many years into the future a value is calculated, but it is often between five and eight years – the typical holding period of a venture capital investor. The valuation at this point is normally then based on relative market multiples (such as price to sales) or comparative transactions of similar-sized companies. Relative methods are used for the exit multiple rather than the perpetual growth method, as the company is almost certainly still going to be in the high growth phase, plus relative value techniques ground the value in what the realisable return is likely to be rather than in a theoretical calculation of what it should be.

Stage 2 – discount exit value to a present value

Once an exit valuation has been projected, step two is to then discount this back to a present value. The discounting process is no different to how cash flows are discounted for a company, only in this instance there is only the one cash flow that needs discounting – the exit value.

$$\text{Company value} = \text{PV of terminal value} = \frac{\text{Exit value}}{(1 + r)^n}$$

The challenge, as you might expect for such a high-risk company, is creating a credible discount rate. As a reminder, the discount rate is made up of three separate components: the risk-free rate (to reflect the opportunity cost), the long-term return of the market (to reflect a reasonable expected return) and the beta (to adjust for company-specific exposure to market risk). These combine to reflect what a rational investor's minimum return expectation should be for a given company.

$$\text{Required return} = \text{Risk-free return} + \beta\,(\text{Expected market return} - \text{Risk-free return})$$

$$\text{Required return} = \text{Risk-free return} + \text{Risk premium}$$

Within this equation, for an early-stage company the risk-free rate is no different to that used by mature company investors, and therefore a long-term government bond is normally used as the input. There is however a difference in risk premium, due to the extreme risk of these investments. While the long-term return for mature companies is around 4%, studies suggest that long-term returns for venture capital have been approximately 20% to 30%, ranging from start-up to early stage. This far higher level of return may sound attractive, but there is a huge dispersion of outcomes around this figure – the return on some holdings is many multiples higher, but in other cases an investment results in a total loss.

The beta, used to adjust the risk premium to make it applicable to a specific company, also needs some modification. For the purpose of mature companies, it is assumed that the beta simply reflects the company's relative systemic risk – its market exposure. For early-stage companies however, it will also need to reflect much of the company-specific risk, as the assumption that an investor can fully diversify across start-ups is unrealistic given the resources and time required for a start-up investment. For example, simply because a biotech company is not heavily exposed to the market, it does not mean that its beta should be below 1 if the company level of risk relative to similar companies is far higher. If this sounds like a bit of a fudge, that is because it is. And while a basic framework is helpful, much of it really comes down to common sense, experience and asking oneself what is a reasonable return given the risks of an investment.

Stage 3 – calculate the post-deal share price

With the post-deal value now calculated for, to conclude on the price per share, the percentage holding that a rational investor would require in return for the investment is first calculated. This is simply determined by dividing the investment amount by the PV of the exit value.

$$\% \text{ required} = \frac{\text{Investment}}{\text{PV of exit value}}$$

Deals are typically reached by negotiation, with the investor wanting a higher portion in exchange for the investment, while existing investors will be reluctant to give too much away. Ultimately, the higher the percentage an investor receives, the lower the implied post-deal valuation. If the percentage holding the investor receives differs from what the required percentage is, the implied post-deal value can be calculated by dividing the investment amount by the percentage received.

$$\text{Implied post-deal value} = \frac{\text{Investment}}{\% \text{ recieved}}$$

Once the percentage of the company that the investor will receive has been determined, the number of new shares that need to be issued can be calculated. This is done by dividing the percentage ownership by one minus that percentage ownership, then multiplying the output by the pre-deal existing share count.

$$\text{New shares} = \frac{\% \text{ ownership}}{1 - \% \text{ ownership}} \times \text{old shares}$$

Added to the existing number of shares outstanding, the sum figure of old and new shares will equal the total post-deal number of shares. This is then divided by the company value to equal the post-deal share price.

$$\text{Price per share} = \frac{\text{Company value}}{\text{Old shares} + \text{New shares}}$$

Example

Investment	\$2 million
Required return	23%
Term	6 years
Exit multiple	15x PE
Exit-year earnings	\$2 million
Existing no. of shares	1 million

Step 1 – calculate exit value

$$\text{Exit Value} = \text{Exit multiple} \times \text{Exit-year earnings}$$

$$\$30 \text{ million} = 15 \times \$2 \text{ million}$$

Step 2 – discount exit value to the present value

$$\text{PV of the exit value} = \frac{\text{Exit value}}{(1 + \text{Required return})^{n}}$$

$$\$8.7 \text{ million} = \frac{\$30 \text{ million}}{(1 + 0.23)^{5}}$$

Step 3 – calculate the post-deal share price

$$\text{Required percentage} = \frac{\text{Invested amount}}{\text{PV of exit value}}$$

$$23\% = \frac{\$2 \text{ million}}{\$8.7 \text{ million}}$$

$$\text{New shares issued} = \frac{\%\text{ ownership}}{1 - \%\text{ ownership}} \times \text{old shares}$$

$$300{,}000 = \frac{23\%}{(1 - 23\%)} \times 1 \text{ million}$$

$$\text{Total outstanding shares} = \text{Old shares} + \text{New shares}$$

$$1{,}300{,}000 = 1{,}000{,}000 + 300{,}000$$

$$\text{Post-deal value per share} = \frac{\text{PV of exit value}}{\text{New shares} + \text{Old shares}}$$

$$\$6.7 \,/\, \text{share} = \frac{\$8.7 \text{ million}}{1.3 \text{ million}}$$

Dealing with dilution

The difficulty with such a valuation is that an early-stage investment round will often mark the start of a company's foray into the financial markets for the capital, rather than the end. The cash drain on early-stage companies can be sizeable, and multiple financing rounds required to plug the cash deficit. Further required investment means more share issuance and the dilution of existing shareholders. This is akin to taking a pizza and slicing it into ever smaller pieces. This leaves early investors with a diminishing sized slice and can reduce once-powerful entrepreneurs to small minority holders in their own company if adjustments are not made. If future capital is likely to be required in order to meet growth targets in the period between investment and exit, the dilution effect needs to be accounted for in the current valuation. This requires a further three steps in addition to the prior process.

Step 1 – develop assumptions

First, dilution assumptions are required to drive the adjustment. There are three key assumptions that need to be made for each round of financing projected: the investment year(s), the investment amount(s) and the discount rate(s). The first two assumptions can be achieved either by a rough guesstimate or, if you are building a model, setting a minimum cash figure for the balance sheet, then assuming a capital raise is required each time the projected cash balance drops below that minimum cash figure. This minimum level should provide the company with a buffer for projection error, and also take into account that management will want to raise money according to its own schedule and not be forced into accepting capital at unattractive terms due to being cash-strapped and out of options.

With regards to the discount rate assumption, funding is always on different terms for each round, as the more the company matures, the more certain its outlook becomes, and consequently, the lower the risk premium required for an investment. Studies have documented that start-up venture discount rates are typically 50-70%, while slightly later-stage venture capital funding is done at a 30-60% discount rate. For instance, the discount rate when the company is little more than a concept may be 70%, but drop to 50% when a prototype has been produced and its outlook is more assured.

The final consideration is the employee share pool – another source of potential future dilution. Company shares are an important means of attracting and retaining talent. They improve alignment and are a cash-free form of remuneration. For this reason, it is not uncommon for a company at an early stage to budget for a targeted amount of employee ownership that it anticipates at exit. This could, for example, be 5% but will likely vary company to company based on their hiring needs and remuneration structures. While this is not a dilution in the traditional sense of equity for capital, an employee ownership at exit assumption does need to be factored into an investor's valuation as it will mean the issuance of future shares, dilution, and therefore reduction in per share value.

Step 2 – calculate the retention rate

For this stage, first calculate the exit-value PV for each financing round using the discount rates and dates specific to that round. You will note that the closer to the exit date the financing round is, the higher the value will be, due to both the declining discount rate and number of periods until exit.

Next, use the investment amount assumption for each particular round and divide it by that round's exit-value PV. This is just the same as step 3 in the pre-dilution method and will equal the minimum percentage that a rational investor should require to participate in a given financing round.

$$\%\text{ required} = \frac{\text{Investment}}{\text{PV of exit value}}$$

Finally, for each individual round, subtract the percentage ownership required from one to equal that round's retention rate.

$$\text{Retention rate} = 1 - (\%\text{ Required})$$

This is the figure that investors prior to that round will 'retain' of the company post-dilution. In the event that there has been an employee ownership assumption created, the retention rate will be equal to one minus the assumption.

Step 3 – adjust the required ownership to reflect the dilution effect

Finally, adjust the initial required ownership for the current financing round by first multiplying all future retention rates together. The output will equal the total amount that an investor will retain upon exit. This figure is then used to calculate the adjusted required ownership, by dividing the pre-dilution required ownership figure by the retention rate output.

$$\text{Adjusted required ownership} = \frac{\text{Pre-dilution required ownership}}{\text{Retention rate}}$$

The adjustment will always increase the pre-dilution figure, and the lower the retention rate, the higher the adjustment upwards. Once this is completed, the steps formerly described to determine the price per share can then be followed – calculate for the number of shares issued, add these to existing shares, then divide the present value of the exit value by total post-deal outstanding shares to equal the price per share.

Example with dilution

Exit year	6
Exit-year earnings	$1,000,000
Exit-year PE multiple	20
Exit-year value	$20,000,000

1. Assumptions

Round	Investment year	Investment amount	Required return
Round 1 (current)	0	$1,000,000	25%
Round 2	2	$1,200,000	20%
Round 3	4	$1,500,000	15%

5% set aside for employee ownership at exit.

2. Retention rate calculations

Round	Present value	Required ownership	Retention rate
Round 1 (current)	5,242,880	19%	
Round 2	11,574,074	10%	90%
Round 3	17,391,304	9%	91%
Employee		5%	95%

3. Adjusted required ownership

Retention rate = 90% × 91% × 95 = 78%

Post-dilution required ownership = 19% ÷ 78% = 24%

Therefore, to invest in round one, the investor would require a minimum 24% ownership in return for the $1,000,000 investment. The final steps to determine the post-deal price are then the same as previously detailed – calculate for the required number of shares issued, add the new shares to the existing shares, then divide the present value of the exit by total post-deal outstanding shares to equal the price per share.

Summary

Valuing a start-up or early-stage company is in principle no different to that of any other company – either relative or intrinsic methods can be employed. However, due to the sheer scale of uncertainty and lack of any type of financial statement inputs to tether a value to, these approaches are commonly adjusted. In the case of relative value, this typically means using absolute values of similar prior transactions rather than ratios for comparison. In the case of intrinsic valuation, it means valuing the investment return rather than the company return to better accommodate for the lack of cash flows and likely dilution. Valuation of any company will never be an exact science. However, start-up and early-stage valuation requires particular caution, as the range of probable outcomes is considerable and any valuation estimate will likely require frequently adjusting as the company develops.

Bank Valuation

Love them or hate them, banks are a critical constituent in the smooth running of any economy, linking those who want to save or invest with those seeking capital. These businesses are largely listed publicly on an exchange and often account for a considerable portion of the listed equity in a country due to their size. For the would-be investor however, they create a number of challenges due to some unique characteristics. While they do not require an investor to wander from key accounting or valuation principles, they do require a difference of approach and additional considerations.

A 'bank' can be involved in a broad range of activities, and for analytical purposes, these require further defining. The key two categories of banks are commercial banks and investment banks. Commercial banks (sometimes known as retail banks) typically serve small businesses and individuals, borrowing low and lending higher. That is, they attract savers to deposit with them by offering an interest return on their deposit, then use that cash to lend to borrowers at a higher rate. The margin the bank makes matching savers with borrowers is then known as the net interest margin.

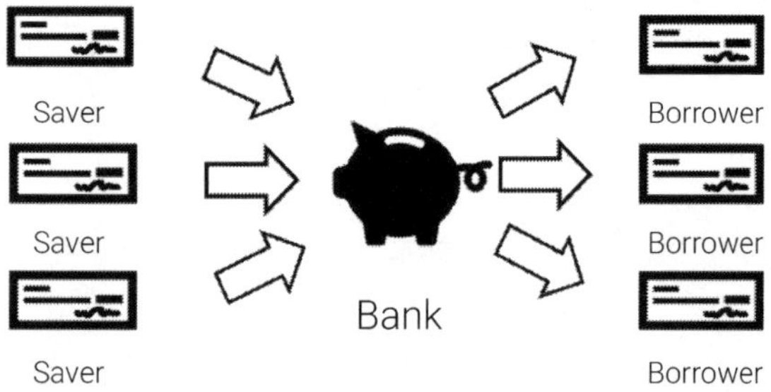

For instance, consider a bank that on average offers 1% on deposits and makes 3% on loans. In this instance, the net interest margin on those loans would be 2% (3% – 1% = 2%). This of course does not sound like much of a margin. However, banks compensate for this by piling on considerable leverage to increase returns to equity – leverage in this case, is largely from deposit liabilities. In addition, interest income is also supplemented by non-interest activity, such as selling other financial products (insurance, funds, etc.) to their customers. In an economy, these businesses are vital to the efficient allocation of capital, allowing savers to save and borrowers to borrow. While they may not be loved, and there are examples of malpractice, these companies have an undeniably important social and economic function.

Investment banks are the second key category of bank. In the past associated with 'casino banking', these companies have historically been far riskier and were indeed broadly blamed for instigating the 2008 financial crisis. Investment banks typically derive the majority of their income from fee-based advisory, often in an intermediary capacity. This can include advising on a merger, helping a company raise capital in the private or public markets, or providing research and a trading platform for institutional asset managers. As part of their business activity, in the past these companies would also commonly leverage their balance sheet to aggressively trade financial securities for their direct gain. This created conflicts of interest with the clients they served, while also leaving them highly exposed to changes in market fortunes. Due to the chaos this caused in 2008, post the financial crisis regulators globally moved to disallow investment banks from taking on sizeable trading risks, and they are now confined to only transacting in the market for the purpose of matching buyers and sellers. This still leaves investment banks exposed, but their risk-taking is now nowhere near the levels that were previously viewed as being part of their operational DNA.

When analysing investment and commercial banks, you need to take a through-the-cycle view of returns and risks. This is often complicated by a changing regulatory landscape and the fact that many of the larger banks are involved in both commercial and investing banking – albeit with these activities ring fenced from one another to contain and isolate risk. For the purpose of this chapter, we are mostly looking at commercial banks and the adjustments required when dealing with interest-bearing assets.

Accounting distinctions

There are a number of important accounting distinctions to be made between banks and non-bank companies. These do not require re-learning accounting principles, only understanding application differences.

From the outset, you will notice that a bank's balance sheet and income statement appear different. For the income statement, the key sales minus expenses equal profit structure is the same. However, the summing lines are different.

Non-bank Income Statement	**Bank Income Statement**
Revenue	Net interest income
Costs	Non interest income
Gross profit	Revenue
Expenses	Provisions
Operating profit	Expenses
Interest	Operating profit
Earnings before Tax	Tax
Tax	Net profit
Net profit	

One important new addition is provisions. This line item reflects expected loss – calculated as the probability of default multiplied by one minus the probable recovery in the event of default. Probability and recovery are combined in unison, as even when a payer cannot make a repayment in full, it is often the case that some of the amount owed can be recouped. For example, in the case of a mortgage, this might include foreclosure and the bank selling the property to recover the loan value.

The provision line is intentionally forward looking, so that costs are recognised parallel to revenue. This is of course consistent with the income statement matching principle covered in the accounting chapter. The outcome of providing at the outset for loss is that in the event of actual loss, the bank does not have to directly reflect that loss through the income statement, as it has already been provisioned for. This therefore significantly smooths earnings through the cycle. In practice however, if a loan is defaulted on, the bank will likely add some additional provisions to provide for the risk of further loss beyond the provisioned amount.

For the balance sheet, the basic structure is the same – assets equal equity plus liabilities. However, there are again differences in terms of what is incorporated in these categories.

Non-bank Balance Sheet

<table>
<tr><td>PP&E</td><td>Debt</td></tr>
<tr><td>Receivables</td><td rowspan="3">Equity</td></tr>
<tr><td>Inventory</td></tr>
<tr><td>Cash</td></tr>
</table>

Bank Balance Sheet

<table>
<tr><td rowspan="2">Loans</td><td>Deposits</td></tr>
<tr><td>Trading liabilities</td></tr>
<tr><td>Trading Assets</td><td>Debt</td></tr>
<tr><td>Federal Funds</td><td rowspan="2">Equity</td></tr>
<tr><td>Cash</td></tr>
</table>

The key differences are the way that loans are presented, and the valuation methodology for marketable securities. In the case of loans, while for most companies debt is a liability representing a future cash outflow, for banks, when debt has been lent with the expectation of a cash inflow to come, it is an asset. When debt is classified as an asset, the loan is recorded on the balance net of the provisions that have been set aside for expected losses. Sometimes it is the case that the calculation for net loans will actually be broken out – so gross loans, minus the allowance for loan and lease losses (provisions recognised through the income statement) will sum for the net loan figure. For example, if the outstanding total loan balance (gross loans) is $100 million and the bank has set aside $1 million of provisions, then the net loan value will be $99 million.

Gross loans	$100,000,000
Allowance for loan and lease losses (ALLL)	$1,000,000
Net loans	$99,000,000

For the purpose of calculating total bank assets, it is then only the net loan figure within this calculation that would be included as an 'asset'. While you will not see this at the individual loan level, in the event that loss actually does occur or a recovery is achieved (losses not as great as feared), this will not directly affect the net loan balance. Instead, in the case of a loss, the gross loan balance declines to the extent of the loss, and the ALLL (allowance for loan and lease losses) simultaneously rises to the same extent. Likewise, in the event of a recovery, the gross loan balance rises and the ALLL drops an equal amount. The net extent of recoveries and losses is known as net charge-offs (losses minus recoveries).

A second notable balance sheet difference is that banks have the option of recognising listed securities at market price rather than amortised cost. The rationale for the difference in accounting treatment is that unlike other assets that can be difficult to value, the price of listed assets such as corporate bonds or government bonds is readily available using transaction data. Moreover, recognising listed securities at market price avoids sudden shocks to the balance sheet if a borrower does default, as the market is considered an efficient discounting mechanism for such risks. Beyond the balance sheet, this also affects the income statement, where all gains and losses must be realised. However, the bank is provided the option of either recognising the loss/gain of a listed security either before net income or only within other comprehensive income. Once a decision is made regarding which option is taken, it must be applied consistently across the securities portfolio, to prevent management manipulating net income. Given the extent of accounting discretion for financial securities, it is well worth understanding which accounting choices have been made and the extent to which they are material to reported operating activity.

Regulation and government oversight

Beyond accounting differences, the role of the regulator also makes banking sector analysis unique. Any industry is regulated, but few are subject to the same degree of government oversight as the banking sector. This is largely due to banks being of systemic significance to an economy, as well as the extensive leverage involved in these companies and the feast or famine nature of their return profile. This has important implications for a bank's leverage, liquidity and liberty, which subsequently affect its value.

With regards to leverage, we have so far utilised leverage ratios that use inputs direct from the balance sheet. For a bank, however, due to the importance that debt plays in returns, a more thorough measurement of leverage is required to adequately capture underlying risk, as not all assets are equally risky. For example, a bank lending to a government would not be equally as risky as one lending to an individual or small company. To reflect this, assets are weighted according to their risk so that a distinction can be made between a bank's conservative and high-risk exposures. The higher the risk, the higher the weight. For instance, cash would have no risk and therefore receive a risk weighting of zero, whereas a mortgage loan has risk and may have a weighting of between 30% and 100%. The weighting is multiplied by the asset to produce what is known as a 'risk-weighted asset' (RWA).

A bank's risk-weighted assets are then put to practical use by regulators and financial analysts by assessing them against a company's equity 'capital'. Just like assets, however, this is also an adjusted figure. The most common adjustment for equity is to transform it into what is known as common equity tier-1 (CET1). This is calculated by taking the balance sheet equity figure and subtracting preferred stock, non-controlling interest and any intangibles (goodwill, etc.). This makes it a more conservative estimation of tangible equity ownership and, when divided by the bank's RWA, it produces a leverage ratio known as the 'tier-1 ratio'.

$$\text{Tier-1 ratio} = \frac{\text{Tier-1 ratio}}{\text{Risk weighted assets}}$$

The higher the ratio, the lower the leverage – this is notably the opposite of our other leverage calculations. For example, a company with \$5 million of tier-1 equity and \$50 million of risk-weighted assets would have a tier-1 ratio of 10%. If its tier-1 equity doubled to \$10 million, the ratio would be a 'safer' 20%.

This ratio is not just important for assessing risk, but also represents a regulatory constraint on leverage, and therefore can limit growth. The most widely assessed set of banking regulations are the Basel accords, a set of international accords created by a broad consortium of central banks to manage banking risk. The most recent of these accords is Basel III, an accord that was created in the wake of the financial crisis and which is used by regulators globally to set leverage and liquidity requirements for banks.

The Basel III accord mandates that tier-1 must be at least 4.5%, and to further guard against the economic cycle a 2.5% buffer applied.

So, in normal times a bank is required to hold 7%, and in periods of economic stress the allowable minimum may drop to 4.5%. In practice however, most banks target to have at least a 10% tier-1 ratio to manage risk. Even this though is equivalent to saying that for every $10 of risk-weighted assets, there is only $1 of equity. Or to put it another way, risk-weighted assets would only need to fall by 10% for equity holders to be wiped out entirely.

While tier-1 is most relevant in terms of risk for common equity shareholders, there are other limitations which may be a constraint on the company. These include 'additional tier-1', which includes preference shares, and tier-2, which extends to subordinated instruments such as convertible bonds and subordinated notes. Both 'other tier-1' and 'tier-2' can also be divided by the company's risk-weighted assets to calculate for alternative leverage ratios regulated by Basel III. Often, a bank's management will in its reporting and presentation emphasise in its disclosure the measure which looks most flattering relative to regulatory requirements. Therefore, it is often worth digging deeper to understand where in practice there may be a limiting constraint.

Beyond risk-adjusted debt constraints, a bank also has liquidity requirements. This is to ensure it always has ample liquidity to meet deposit withdrawals to avoid a 'run on the bank'. This is known as the reserve rate requirement and is calculated by dividing reserves maintained at the central bank by deposits. The higher the figure, the easier it is for the bank to meet withdrawals. For regulatory purposes, this is typically between 10% and 15% for banks. In some countries, such as China, the central bank actively adjusts the reserve requirement to manage liquidity in the economy, increasing it when it seeks to reduce inflation and decreasing it when it wants to encourage growth.

The final difference is liberty. Due to the level of impact these banks have on society, everything from M&A to lending practices is often under scrutiny, limiting their liberty to operate as they might like. Constraints range from policies to limit any group of banks becoming 'too big to fail', to active regulator involvement in risk-taking parameters.

It is sometimes the case that governments even have direct ownership in banks. This can have a considerable impact on the banks' priorities. Sometimes ownership is a consequence of a bank's strategic importance to the government, which wants to primarily use the bank to promote policy – as often seen in emerging market countries. In this example, shareholder return will likely not be the key consideration when decision making. Some governments also have holdings in banks as a legacy of the 2008 financial crisis, when equity injections by governments made them reluctant owners. In this case, there is a greater likelihood that the government will want to create shareholder value and ideally at some point exit via a share sale.

Key assumptions

The key determinants that affect a bank's outlook are loan and deposit growth, the net interest margin, credit costs and non-interest income. There are of course other assumptions that will be required, such as non-interest expenses and the effective tax rate, but these are often less volatile and/or less material to the company's outlook.

Loans

Loans are in effect the product that the bank is selling, while deposits are the cost. Loan growth assumptions can be developed in a similar way to sales assumptions – by combining the outlook of market growth and market share to derive a sales figure, or, more simply, just projecting a headline growth figure. Often however, due to loan demand's sensitivity to economic activity, it is linked to GDP growth by calculating historic GDP growth to loan growth as a multiple (dividing the two) and then applying that multiple to a future GDP growth assumption. For example, if GDP was expected to grow 3% over the next four years and a bank's loan growth had historically been 1.3 times the GDP growth rate, the projected loan growth could be calculated as 3% x 1.3 = 3.9%.

With loan growth calculated for, we can, due to the close and typically stable relationship between loans and deposits, use the outstanding projected loan balance to then calculate for the deposit amount. This is done by using the loan to deposit ratio (loans divided by deposits). As a percentage, this is typically between 60% and 100%, although it can be higher. When the loan value is divided by the loan to deposit ratio, it provides the projected deposit value. For example, if a company had historically had a loan to deposit ratio of 80%, there was no reason to believe this should change in the future and the projected loan figure was $500 million, this would equate to a deposit estimate of $625 million for that period ($500 million ÷ 80% = $625 million).

Net interest income

Net interest income is the next key variable. This is calculated as interest income minus interest on deposits. This will require assumptions regarding the average loan and deposit yield over a period. To compute yields to analyse past trends, in the case of loans we calculate this by dividing interest income by the average loan balance. For deposits, we divide interest expense by the average deposit balance.

$$\text{Asset yield} = \frac{\text{Interest income}}{\text{Average interest bearing assets}}$$

$$\text{Deposit cost} = \frac{\text{Interest expense}}{\text{Average deposits}}$$

Bear in mind that interest rates do change over time, so look at recent changes in interest rates to help determine if you should be adjusting future periods up or down. This assumption will be used for the income statement calculation of interest income and expense, by being multiplied by the balance sheet loan and deposit amount. So, using the prior example, if the loan balance was $500 million and the interest rate 4%, that would equal interest income of $20 million.

Credit costs

The third key variable is the credit costs – the loan loss provisions detailed earlier. Based on expected loss rather than realised loss, the assumption is a percentage ratio that for past periods can be calculated by dividing the credit loss line by the current and prior-period loan balance average. It will typically be a low single-digit figure, for example between 0.5% and 3%. Forward-looking assumptions are best based on past averages, and often need adjusting up or down based on your own judgement. For instance, if you believe there will be an economic downturn or that the bank has recently been making carelessly risky loans, a revision up from the average will likely be required.

Non-interest income

The final key variable, non-interest income, is typically dominated by fee and commission activity, such as bank card fees, remittance fees, commission on financial products sold, etc. The assumption for this is normally calculated as a percentage of gross loans outstanding for commercial banks. For investment banks though, it is better projected using a growth assumption tied to your view on their prospects. Ultimately, this will likely be a very cyclical line on the income statement.

Others

Other assumptions are important, although they are either less variable or have a limited impact on returns. Non-interest expenses are typically dominated by those related to staff, IT, general and administrative and rental. These are normally calculated as a percentage growth figure, or as a percentage of net revenue.

Modelling

Developing a financial model for a bank requires the same basic steps as for a non-bank:

1. Input and format historical data
2. Detail assumptions
3. Set up supporting schedules
4. Link up the financial statements.

The first stage should be similar to the process for a non-bank company – namely, inputting historical data, calculating historic ratios and, importantly, simplifying the statements by combining certain similar line items together. Taking time to do this step properly will save you time later.

Once formatting has been completed, the assumptions need to be developed. You will notice that there is a greater emphasis on balance sheet assumptions for a bank valuation, and that many of the assumptions are quite different from those for a non-bank. Some of the more variable and material assumptions have already been covered. In other cases, it is typically reasonable to use long-run averages in the absence of any particular insight into why a trend or level may change.

As with non-bank companies, first calculate the historic figures for these assumptions to help inform your forward projections. In each case where a calculation is made that includes both a balance sheet item and income statement item, ensure you use the average of the current and prior year for the balance sheet input. This is required, as performance using average assets is far more accurate than performance based simply on the end-of-period figure, and especially so in the case of growth companies.

Balance sheet assumptions

Loan growth	YoY % Growth
Loan to deposit ratio (LDR)	Loans ÷ Deposits
Net charge-offs	% of average Gross loans
Capital asset turnover	Sales ÷ Average PP&E
Depreciation expense	% of Sales
Trading assets	% of Deposits
Other assets	% of Assets
Trading liabilities	% of Deposits
Other liabilities	% of Deposits
Long-term debt	Local currency amount outstanding
Pref. share issuance	Local currency amount outstanding
Common stock issuance	Local currency amount outstanding
Risk-weighted assets percentage	Risk-weighted assets ÷ Interest-earning assets

Income statement assumptions

Interest-earning asset (IEA) yield	Interest income ÷ Average interest-earning assets
Deposit cost	Interest expense ÷ Average deposits
Non-interest income	YoY % growth
Provision for credit cost	Provision for credit cost ÷ Average gross loans
Non-interest expense	YoY or % of Sales
Effective tax rate	Tax ÷ Earnings before tax
Dividend	% of Net income

The supporting schedules are then set up. For a bank, there will be three supporting schedules: the loan loss schedule, the net interest income schedule and the depreciation schedule. These are used so that you do not have to perform detailed calculations in a single cell, thereby reducing the chance of error. With the exception of the depreciation schedule however, these for the moment will only be set up, as they will require the gross loan figure to complete.

The net loan supporting schedule

The net loan schedule is developed for the purpose of deriving a net loan and provision figure. First, the ending allowance for loan losses is calculated by inputting the prior-year balance sheet reserve balance, then adding current period net charge-offs plus additions to provisions. The balance sheet net loan figure is then calculated for by calculating for gross loans, then deducting the ending allowance for loan loss provisions calculated.

Prior allowance for loan losses	Prior period ending balance
Net charge-offs	Net charge-offs (a) × Gross loans
Addition to provisions	Provision (a) × Gross loans
Ending allowance for loan losses	Prior period + Net charge-offs + Addition to provisions
Gross loans	Prior period × (1 + Growth (a))
Loan loss provisions	Ending allowance for loan losses (ss)
Net loans	Gross loans – Loan loss provisions

The interest income supporting schedule

The interest income supporting schedule is then set up, to derive the income statement net interest income figure. This is developed by first calculating for total interest-earning assets (IEA). These include not just loans, but any other income-yielding asset – namely, bonds in investment securities. Note also that gross loans are calculated as 'cumulative' net of charge-offs (actually experienced loss). Cumulative charge-offs are calculated by summing all prior charge-offs in the projection period.

Once interest-earning assets have been calculated for, next multiply the output by the interest-earning asset yield assumption to derive interest income. Similarly, for deposits, multiply by the deposit interest assumption to derive the interest expense. The interest income and interest expense are then summed to equal the net interest income.

Step 1	
Gross loans	Gross loans × (1 + Loan growth (a))
Gross loans net of charge-offs	Gross loans – Cumulative charge-offs*
Other interest-earning assets	Any other investment securities
Total interest-earning assets (IEA)	Gross loans net of charge-offs + Other IEA
Step 2	
Interest income	IEA (ss) × IEA yield (a)
Interest expense	Deposits × Deposit cost (a)
Net interest income	Interest income – Interest expense

**Cumulative charge-offs are calculated by summing all prior charge-offs in the projection period*

The PP&E supporting schedule

Finally, as per non-bank financial modelling, the depreciation schedule is developed. This will provide the CAPEX and depreciation expense for the cash flow statement, plus the PPE balance for the balance sheet. You will note that for banks, PP&E is proportionally far smaller on the balance sheet than for the typical non-bank company.

Beginning of period PP&E	Prior period end balance
Capital expenditures	End of period PP&E (ss) + Depreciation expense (ss) - Beginning PP&E (ss)
Depreciation expense	Sales × Depreciation expense (a)
End of period PP&E	Sales ÷ Capital asset turnover (a)

With our assumptions and schedules complete or set up, the financial statements can now be solved for. As with the non-bank financial model, this comes down to linking cells. Start with the balance sheet, as this will drive income statement projections, which in turn will help develop the cash flow statement. You will note that within the balance sheet, assets such as central bank funds, investment securities, and others are all connected with deposits – the rationale being that all these asset line items require funding from deposits. As deposits are a derivative of our loan growth assumption, this makes loan growth the key variable that drives much of the balance sheet.

Balance sheet

Cash	Prior period + Net change in cash (CF statement)
Central bank funds	Deposits × Central bank funds (a)
Investment securities	Deposits × Investment securities (a)
Trading assets	Deposits × Trading assets (a)
Net loans	Net loans (ss)
PP&E	PP&E (ss)
Goodwill	Hold stable
Other assets	Deposits × Other assets (a)
Assets	Sum asset lines
Deposits	Loans ÷ LDR (a)
Trading liabilities	Assets × Trading assets
Long-term debt	LT debt (a)
Other liabilities	Deposits × Other liabilities (a)
Liabilities	Sum liabilities lines
Preferred stock	Preferred stock (a)
Common stock	Common stock (a)
Retained earnings	Prior period + Net income – Dividends
Equity	Sum equity lines

Remember that for the moment the balance sheet will not be completed, and therefore it will not yet balance. On the asset side, cash can only be completed once the cash flow statement is finalised, while within equity, retained earnings can only be completed once the income statement is finished.

Income statement

The income statement for a bank is the next financial statement to focus on. First however, use the completed balance sheet to complete the net interest income support schedule, as the output will be needed. As with the balance sheet, the complexity of the income statement will really come down to the extent to which you have simplified it. Below is a heavily simplified example.

Non-interest income	% growth rate (a)
Net interest income	Net interest income (ss) output
Revenue	Non-interest + net interest income
Provision for credit losses	Provisions (ss)
Non-interest expense	Revenue × Expense ratio (a)
Pre-tax income	Revenue - Provisions - Expenses
Taxes	Pre-tax income × Tax rate (a)
Net income	Pre-tax income - Taxes

Cash flow statement

The cash flow statement follows the same type of steps as for a non-bank, largely simply unwinding the accrual accounting within the income statement and balance sheet. Most financial analysts however, when forecasting a banks outlook for the purpose of valuation, will not forecast for the cash flow statement as it does not feature in the valuation process. None the less, the cash flow forecasting details are provided below, if you want to build it for the purpose of analysis.

Net income	Input from income statement
Provision for credit losses	Input from income statement
Depreciation	Depreciation (ss)
Investment securities	−(Current period - Prior period)
Trading assets	−(Current period - Prior period)
Other assets	−(Current period - Prior period)
Trading liabilities	(Current period - Prior period)
Other liabilities	(Current period - Prior period)
Cash flow from operations (CFO)	Sum CFO lines
Central bank funds	−(Current period - Prior period)
Gross loans	−(Current period - Prior period)
Capital expenditure	−(Input from (ss))
Cash flow from investing (CFI)	Sum CFI lines
Deposits	Current period - Prior period
Long-term debt	Current period - Prior period
Common stock	Current period - Prior period
Preferred stock	Current period - Prior period
Dividends	−(Div. payout (a) × Net income)
Cash flow from financing (CFF)	Sum CFF lines
Net change in cash	= CFO + CFI + CFF

With the cash flow statement completed, go back to the balance sheet and complete the balance sheet cash figure by adding the net change in cash to the prior-year cash balance. If all has been inputted correctly, then the balance sheet should balance exactly.

Once the model is complete and working, we should calculate regulatory- and profitability-related ratios to provide insight into whether our assumptions are reasonable. These allow us to step back and look at the company in terms of end outcome, and to adjust assumptions in the event that these create a management response. If, for example, the output of the models shows that return on equity is below what would be reasonably required of equity for the bank, then it may make us question the extent to which management wish to grow the loan book. Similarly, if capital ratios drop below regulatory or management targets, we should reconsider assumptions regarding dividend distributions and/or share issuance amounts.

Return on equity	Net income ÷ Average book equity
Return on assets	Net income ÷ Average book assets
Net interest margin	Interest income ÷ Average loans
Provision ratio	Provision for losses ÷ Average net loans
Assets to equity	Assets ÷ Equity
Tier-1 equity	Tier-1 equity ÷ Risk-weighted assets

Valuation

For a bank, it is extremely hard to separate operating, investing and financing activities. For most non-banks, for instance, debt issuance may be a means of funding the business in general. For a bank, however, debt issuance is a specific part of the operational process to generate interest income. Therefore, when carrying out a discounted cash flow valuation, there are difficulties when using free cash flow to the firm or free cash flow to equity. As a consequence, it is best to use dividends for the cash flow component and required return on equity for the discount rate.

This means that ensuring a realistic dividend payout ratio assumption (the portion of earnings paid as a dividends) is particularly important.

Both the bank's capability and willingness to distribute a dividend need to be assessed. This latter point is especially important in cases where the government is a significant stakeholder and may put pressure on the board to prioritise lending over delivering an otherwise rational shareholder return policy. Often, the dividend payout ratio for a bank is relatively stable. However, there will always be a balance between using cash to strengthen the balance sheet (lowering leverage), growing the balance sheet (making loans), and making distributions to shareholders (dividends).

Another form of effective shareholder return is a share buyback, and indeed for some companies this can be the primary means of capital return. While a share buyback does not distribute cash directly to investors, it does reduce the number of shares outstanding, thereby increasing the per share dividend distribution. Therefore, when seeking to understand actual per share dividend payments, ensure to incorporate any buyback plans into your analysis or forecast.

For relative value, the three most commonly used ratios are the price to earnings (PE) multiple, the price to book (PB) multiple, and the dividend yield. This is consistent with non-bank equivalents, although typically there is a far greater emphasis on the PB multiple for a bank. The PB multiple is favoured largely due to its applicability throughout the cycle, making it easily comparable across time as well as across company. In addition, book equity value for banks is a reasonable starting point, as banking assets tend to be largely tangible and included on the balance sheet (unlike in the case of consumer, healthcare or tech companies).

While the book value is a relatively stable anchor for a valuation, due to the leverage that banks employ, large write-downs can still be required during times of deep economic stress, as was the case during the 2008 banking crisis. The multiple therefore needs to be very much considered in the context of the economic cycle. Indeed, to be conservative, many professional analysts only include the tangible book value of the bank when calculating for 'equity'. The tangible book value (TBV) can be preferable as it includes only what common shareholders can expect to receive if a firm went bankrupt. It is calculated as the equity book value of the company minus any intangible assets. In most cases, the only possible intangible asset of any significance on a bank's balance sheet will be goodwill.

We can also use an adjusted dividend discount model to estimate a fair PB multiple for a bank, independent of peer valuations. This is calculated by dividing return on equity (ROE) minus growth (g) by the required return on equity (r) minus growth.

$$\textbf{PB} = \frac{\text{ROE} - g}{r - g}$$

For this equation, the ROE will need to be the long-term, through-the-cycle, sustainable ROE, while the required return on equity will be its through-the-cycle average. The growth assumption (g) can be derived either by rough estimate or by calculating it as the ROE multiplied by the retention ratio (one minus the dividend payout).

$$\text{Growth} = \text{ROE} \times (1 - \text{dividend payout ratio})$$

This growth assumption is based on the premise that earnings not paid out in dividends will be reinvested and achieve the sustainable return on equity. This assumption is normally preferable, as it reflects a growth rate that is feasible over the long term, given the level of dividend payout.

While this equation is very sensitive to its inputs, the key relationship is between the return on equity and the required return on equity. The greater the spread between these two figures, the higher the multiple. For example, if growth was assumed to be zero and the return on equity was equal to the required return, then the bank should trade at exactly book value. If, however, that same bank was to achieve a through-the-cycle equity return in excess of its required return, then it should trade at a premium to book value (and likewise a discount if equity returns were lower). The growth component within the equation then exaggerates the premium or discount – meaning if the required return is above the return on equity, the bank should lower the dividend payout (and hence increase growth), whereas if it is above, then it should raise it (and lower growth).

The below is an example of how the PB multiple is used in practice:

Required return on equity	7%
Return on equity	9%
Dividend payout	60%
Equity book value	$5 billion

$$\text{Growth: } 2.8\% = 7\% \times (1 - 60\%)$$

$$\text{PB multiple} = 1.47 = \frac{9\% - 2.8\%}{7\% - 2.8\%}$$

$$\text{Company value} = \$7.3 \text{ billion} = \$5 \text{ billion} \times 1.47$$

Summary

Banks are among the most difficult companies to value due to their highly cyclical nature and their reliance on accrual assumptions around future loss. When developing a financial model for a bank, bear in mind that it is very much balance sheet driven – unlike a non-bank, which is typically driven by its income statement assumptions. When performing intrinsic valuation, the dividend discount model is the most appropriate due to issues with using free cash flow to the firm or equity. For relative value, the price to book multiple is the most commonly relied on due to its applicability through the cycle and the largely tangible nature of a bank's asset value.

PROFIT

Profiting from Insights

'Knowledge is of no value unless you put it into practice' – Anton Chekhov

Valuation in itself is but a means to an end. For most people conducting company valuation, that end will be an investment decision – buy or sell. That is, if the current price that the company is transacting at is lower than the fair value you have calculated, it is undervalued and therefore a 'buy'. If it is higher, then it is overvalued and a 'sell'.

In practice of course, if you are looking at a number of companies and only seeking a single investment, then opportunities can be ranked by their upside to fair value. The greater the percentage difference between fair value and price, the greater the opportunity to profit. So for example, while being mindful of the risks involved, a company with 45% upside would be preferable to one with only 10%. The principle to fundamental investing is that the market price over time – be it minutes, days, months or even years – should then converge to fair value. As well-known investor Benjamin Graham famously said, 'In the short run the market is a voting machine, in the long run it is a weighing machine'. This is true across any manner of company, no matter its industry or size, quality or growth outlook.

For companies that are private, transacting can take time and be cumbersome. Individual investors are therefore rarely involved. Public companies that are listed on a stock exchange can be bought and sold multiple times in a day using an online brokerage account. This brings investing in scope for virtually anyone. No matter if you have $100 or $100 million, you can set yourself up and be ready to participate in the market within hours.

If a company has upside, that is simple enough. But what happens when you want to profit from an anticipated fall in a price (a company that is overvalued)? That becomes harder, but is not impossible. It is achieved through a process known as short-selling – the stock is 'shorted'. To do this, the investor borrows the target company's stock from existing shareholders via a broker, sells it in the open market and pockets the cash. Then when that investor wants to close-out the short sell, he or she buys the target company's shares in the market and returns them to the shareholder. The profit or loss of that transaction will be equal to the price at which it is sold minus the price at which it was bought (plus any broker fees).

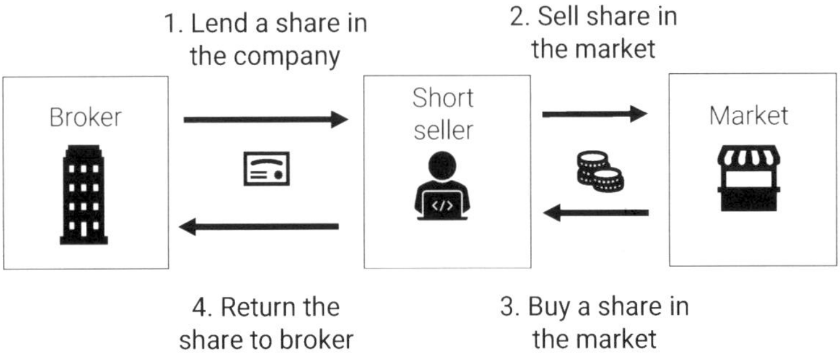

For example, imagine you wanted to short one share of Apple, which was then trading at $135. You would first go to a broker and borrow an existing shareholder's share. Then, you would immediately sell it in the market and pocket the $135 proceeds from that sale. Imagine then that the price later dropped from $135 to $85 and you wanted to close out the short sale. You would then purchase the Apple stock in the market at $85 per share and return it to the broker. Your profit before any fees in this transaction would be $50 – the $135 cash that you received when selling it, minus the $85 that you had to pay to purchase it back. In this transaction, had the share price of Apple risen, you would have paid the difference and endured a loss.

Short selling is often deeply frowned upon as being somehow unethical. In practice though, it contributes to making the market more efficient and is another form of price discovery. If a company was not shorted and its share price was considerably overvalued, capital could potentially be misallocated as its cost of equity would be understated.

Identifying companies to value

There are thousands of listed companies, and an investor may have to 'kiss plenty of frogs' before identifying an attractive opportunity. This makes having a structured approach for identifying potential investment candidates an important part in the investment process.

Professional investors working in venture capital or private equity often use subscription services such as Pitchbook for information on private companies, where information is harder to come by. Pitchbook collates multiple sources to provide details on, amongst other things, the company's profile, management profiles, board information, funding history and deals, as well as other data from the news and public records such as financial details. Opportunities can then be screened by characteristics such as size or sector to reduce the investment universe down to a manageable number of potential investment prospects.

Most public market professionals, such as those typically found at asset management firms, use Bloomberg to screen through opportunities. Bloomberg is a platform which aggregates data across nearly all companies so that they are easily comparable. As with private market tools, screens can be created to rank listed names. For a 'growth investor' this might involve ranking the investment universe by three-year historic sales growth figures, for example. For a 'quality' investor, it might include criteria that emphasise profitability, such as return on equity. For a value investor, the emphasis would be on valuation metrics such as price to earnings. It is often the case that a combination of characteristics will be used – for example, reducing the investment universe by inputting the following screening criteria:

- Companies in the US with a market cap of over $5 billion
- Companies with an ROE in excess of 10%
- Companies with net debt to equity below 5%
- Companies with three-year historic earnings growth of over 15%
- Companies with a PE multiple below 20x

The more measures that are used to screen a company against, the shorter the list will be. Screening for opportunities should however always be only a starting point, as there can be a myriad of reasons for a company to screen well and appear quantitively attractive but in practice be a bad investment opportunity.

For individuals, it is more difficult. A subscription to either PitchBook or Bloomberg costs around $20,000 per year, putting it beyond scope for most. As a very general rule, an alternative good starting point is to focus on companies operating in a space that you know or are interested in. For example, if you work in the automotive industry, why not consider Tesla? Or if you like gaming, you could perhaps look at a gaming company such as Blizzard or eSports. In reality though, many of us have pretty mundane jobs or interests, which may not align with real world opportunities. Therefore, it is best to combine understanding and interest with a 'where the money is at' mentality.

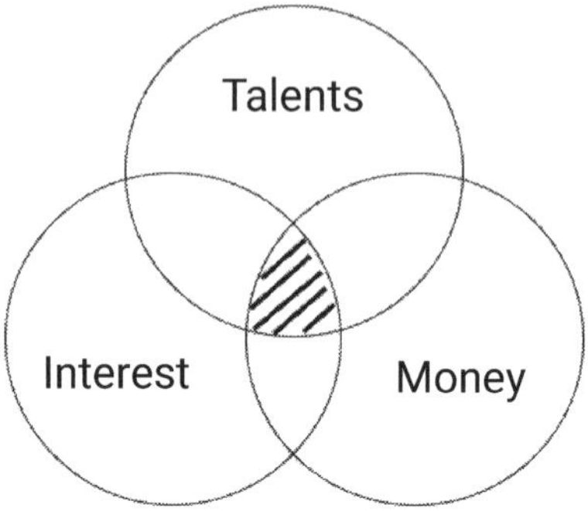

While not included in the chart above, values are also an important element to consider for many investors. Ultimately, remember that when you invest you become an owner – and with that, you share in the company's responsibility to society and the environment. If you do not believe in what a company is doing and do not think that you can effect change at it, there are plenty of other opportunities out there. Therefore, as a rule, it is best to move on.

Finally, enjoy it! While valuing and investing in a company may appear at first sight to be a very process-driven, it absolutely should be fun – once you have got your head round the key concepts. This is especially so for the curious, the competitive and those who like solving puzzles. Being able to invest with confidence brings a tremendous sense of fulfilment, not to mention monetary benefits when you also profit from those actions.

Summary

To quote famed investor Benjamin Graham again, 'Investors should purchase stocks like they purchase groceries, not like they purchase perfume.' That is certainly not to say that you should not consider high-growth, exciting opportunities, only that you must always be disciplined and objective, no matter the company being valued. Understanding what makes an opportunity under- or over-valued, is a very simple but critical component to making money from your valuation insight.

Beyond the actual 'deal or no deal' decision, scouring a huge universe of potential investment candidates can of course be daunting. However, it need not be, as long as you can develop a screening approach to reduce the number of potential names down to a manageable level. For professionals, that might include quantitative tools such as PitchBook or Bloomberg, although individuals will likely focus upon a nexus of what they are good at, what they are passionate about and what makes money.

Avoiding Behavioural Biases

"Investing success doesn't correlate with IQ after you're above a score of 25. Once you have ordinary intelligence, then what you need is the temperament to control urges that get others into trouble" – Warren Buffett

Are you rational? Perhaps you think so, but the likelihood is that in certain situations you are not. Ever met a parent who thought they had an ugly baby, for instance? So far, for the purpose of valuation, we have assumed that investors are rational beings – ones that prefer higher returns and less risk, demonstrate self-control and are not confused or affected by bias. Of course, however, that is rarely the case, not least when faced with the excitement of investing and prospect of making a profit. None of us are a clean slate when it comes to analysis. We each carry our own personal baggage to the process and this can severely weigh down our ability to make sound judgements and draw rational conclusions.

Behavioural biases can be both a weakness and an advantage. They no doubt negatively affect an investor's ability to make rational choices. However, the market chaos and confusion this flaw creates is also the reason why there is ample opportunity for a savvy investor to make abnormal profits beyond what traditional finance theory would suggest is possible in an 'efficient market'.

To do that though, these biases must first be understood. Many biases have been identified through research and studies and they are usually loosely categorised as being either cognitive or emotional. Some of the most important ones are listed below.

Cognitive bias

Cognitive bias refers to types of errors in thinking that occur when we're processing and interpreting information. These are generally 'rules of thumb' or 'mental shortcuts' that help us make sense of the world and reach decisions quickly. While these shortcuts can help us to manage large amounts of information, investors often overly rely on generalisations and therefore overlook when change takes place.

Anchoring

Psychologists have found that people tend to rely too heavily on the very first piece of information they learn. This is known as 'anchoring'. This is why, for example, negotiators often start with an extreme demand to anchor expectation, then make small, slow concessions to reach a preferred outcome. It is likewise the reason why so many of us are drawn to 'discounts', irrespective of what an objective value placed on an item may have been.

For investors, there are various ways that anchoring commonly manifests. For example, historical values, such as an acquisition price or high-water mark, are common anchors that investors attach undue importance to. For instance, if shares in a company were purchased at $10 (the anchor), the individual might consider $12 'expensive' and $8 'cheap', overlooking the company's longer-term price range or any type of bottom-up built understanding of value.

Conservatism

Conservatism is when an analyst maintains a prior view or forecast, despite new information to the contrary. We likely all know someone who resists or fails to accept change. Investors too are frequently overly set in their beliefs and opinions, failing to change even when circumstances do. This bias often means that change is slow to be priced into a company's share piece. Companies considered 'blue chip' and high quality, for example, can in some cases have years of poor performance before it is at last recognised in their valuation. Likewise, historically weak companies that have turned around and are now delivering good performance can be stubbornly undervalued as investors struggle to shake off past perceptions. For those who can understand and adapt when change takes place, there are often attractive opportunities for positions to be exited or entered before the broader market prices that change in.

Confirmation bias

Confirmation bias describes the natural human penchant to seek or emphasise information that confirms an existing conclusion. This impacts how we gather information, but also influences how we interpret and recall information. For example, people who support or oppose a particular issue will not only typically seek information to support it, but will also interpret news stories in a way that upholds their existing ideas and will remember details in a way that reinforces these attitudes. This is notable during an election, for example, when many sit in an echo chamber of similar opinions, reinforcing, reiterating and accentuating a prior belief. Indeed, companies such as Facebook know that this is such a strong human characteristic that they have set algorithms to provide an individual with content that supports their existing biases, therefore making the content more likely to be consumed.

Investors equally are often guilty of seeking information to reinforce an existing belief and, as a consequence, can miss important information or misinterpret evidence. We can see evidence of this bias in everything from the research we decide to consume to the facts that we look for. Indeed, when there is an opportunity to ask questions direct to management, studies suggest that rather than keeping questions open-ended and being open-minded, investors often frame their questions with the intention – conscious or not – of receiving a desired response.

Oversimplification

Albert Einstein famously said, "Make things as simple as possible, but no more simple." The same should hold true for investors, but it often does not. All too often, in seeking to comprehend complex matters, a simple explanation is sought. However, some matters are inherently complicated and cannot be boiled down to a simple sentence or variable. Nuance and context are all too often in short supply, and misunderstandings can quickly develop into errors of judgement.

Companies are complex, and while it is always important to ensure that the wood is not missed for the trees, it is also important to not be blinkered by oversimplification. For example, it would be an error to simply attribute Amazon's success to the rise of online retail. Such an analysis would not just misinterpret the past, but also heighten the risk of error when forecasting the future.

Herd mentality

Herd mentality is a term drawn from the animal kingdom. It describes when people do something primarily or partly because others are doing it. They jump on the bandwagon. Take shopping in the sales, for example. Studies have found that the experience is actually enhanced when there are large crowds. What objectively may be a bad idea becomes a good idea as others are doing it.

While this may sound childish, it is all too evident in equity markets. Financial analysts feel reassured when others are drawing the same conclusion as them and are therefore more likely to follow consensus thinking. Herd mentality can exaggerate movements in the market, as consensus beliefs compound into a circular confirmation loop and markets become unhinged from fundamentals, creating extreme peaks and troughs. Warren Buffett has spoken in the past how he avoids this particular bias by being 'greedy when others are fearful and fearful when others are greedy'.

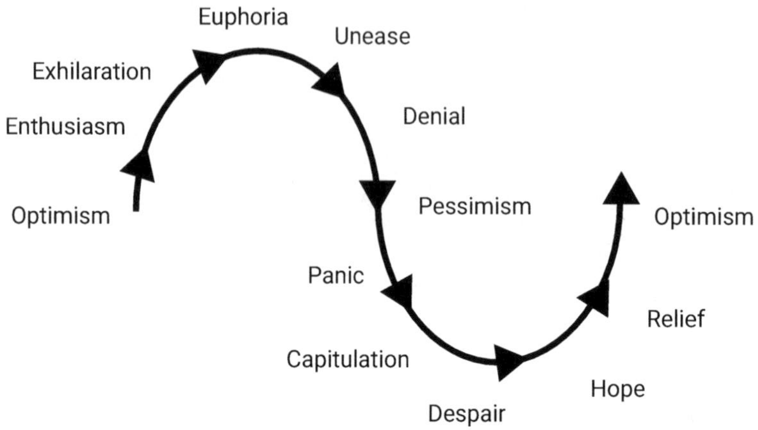

Availability bias

Availability bias is when undue emphasis is put on the information that is readily available. It occurs when individuals judge the probability of an event occurring by the ease with which it comes to mind. It is therefore often the case that more recent events are typically easier to recall than past or distant memories, leading us to overweight recent history and be more likely to neglect the more distant past. One classic example of availability bias is the tendency of most people to guess that shark attacks cause fatalities more frequently than airplane parts falling from the sky. In reality, however, airplane parts falling from the sky are thirty times more likely to be the cause of death than a shark attack. This misperception is largely due to recallability – shark attacks create a more entrenched memory and receive a disproportionate degree of media attention given their frequency.

When valuing a company, availability bias creates an increased risk of forecasting error. This can be particularly acute for financial professionals who are expected to digest substantial amounts of information when assessing opportunities. It can also add to the volatility of markets, as investors become overly complacent in a rising market and over-panic when caught up in a collapsing one. In both cases, long-term perspective is often lost in the moment.

EMOTIONAL BIAS

Emotional biases are due to psychological predispositions. They are based on the personal feelings of an individual at the time the decision is made, creating a spontaneous rather than rational response. This form of bias can be particularly damaging and is often harder to overcome than cognitive bias as it is so intrinsically hard-wired into who a person is. You only need to look at the volatility of the markets to be reminded of our animal instincts and susceptibility to emotional influences.

Loss aversion

Loss aversion bias arises when an individual is particularly loathed to take an action that will realise a loss, even when that action is rational. For example, have you ever taken a wrong turn and, despite knowing that turning back will be the quickest course of action, instead stubbornly ploughed on? Investors are much the same. They resent admitting to themselves that they have made a loss. Therefore, rather than selling a stock that has declined, they are far more likely to hold onto it and hope for a turnaround, even if the evidence suggests that is unlikely. In their subconscious, they rationalise that a loss somehow does not count until the investment has been sold and the loss monetised. The outcome is that it is common for investors to hold onto a company with losses for too long and suffer simply because they cannot accept defeat.

Regret aversion

As the name suggests, regret aversion refers to being afraid of taking action because you don't want to regret being wrong. This might apply to a spontaneous purchase on a limited time offer as you do not want to regret later not making the purchase, or to going out with friends when you would rather stay at home, in order to not regret missing out. While sometimes this may help inform a rational decision, it can often cloud objective judgement.

For investors, regret aversion occurs as either a fear of commission (acting when they shouldn't) or omission (failing to act when they should). In the case of the former, this is manifested when the fear of committing to an investment and being wrong leads to an irrationally high level of risk perception being placed on that investment. As a result, otherwise attractive opportunities are sometimes avoided. The fear of omission is similar to FOMO – fear of missing out – when we chase after a market for fear of regret if we miss out on the opportunity. This can lead to bubbles, as a rising market attracts more investors who don't want to regret missing out – an effect that can quickly compound prices to irrational highs.

Overconfidence

Overconfidence is the belief that we are better than we are actually are. Studies have shown that this is a prevalent human trait, with one survey, for example, finding that 76% of Americans believe they are above average at driving, despite 93% admitting to unsafe behaviour. We have a natural tendency to overestimate our capability.

While for investors having confidence and being decisive can be a strength, it more often leads to unnecessary estimation errors. This includes 'over ranking' (taking too much risk down to an excessive belief in one's capability), 'timing optimism' (underestimating how long it takes to get tasks done) and 'desirability effect' (overestimating the odds of an outcome simply because it is desirable).

Managing biases

Fortunately, there are ways to be avoid being held hostage to one's biases. The first – as any rehabilitation clinic will tell you – is to recognise you have a problem. Accepting you are fallible, understanding your behavioural biases, and being cognisant of the ways these will likely affect you can help you avoid making such behavioural errors in the future. When creating assumptions, for example, ask yourself if the evidence really supports the view taken, and whether an entirely rational investor would draw the same conclusions. The answers can often be surprising.

Next, ensure that your research follows a logical and repeatable decision-making process. Process should be a priority over outcome for an investor, in order to reach objective conclusions. The court, castle and moat approach is one such example of a systematic methodology to analyse a target company using a consistent framework of factors. Once a set of conclusions has been drawn, the rationale should be clearly audited, and updated when new information becomes available.

Finally, challenge your assumptions – or ideally have someone look through your investment case and play devil's advocate. This might be uncomfortable, as we have a natural tendency to avoid confrontation and slip into 'group think'. However, having a challenge process forces any analysis to confront the status quo and properly assess areas that might otherwise be overlooked due to behavioural biases. Charlie Munger, Vice Chairman of Berkshire Hathaway and Warren Buffett's business partner, famously said: "Rapid destruction of your ideas when the time is right is one of the most valuable qualities you can acquire. You must force yourself to consider arguments on the other side."

Summary

Behavioural biases plague all of us. Whether in our everyday life or when it comes to financial analysis, we are all fallible. These biases can loosely be categorised as either cognitive or emotional, and include a range of irrational actions that run contrary to the assumption that markets are driven by rational investors. Preventive measures to limit the impact of these biases include understanding how they might impact analysis, ensuring that analysis is process driven, not being afraid to challenge one's assumptions, and accepting criticism.

Remember, the valuation and investment process might be part art and part science; it should however always be objective, no matter your background, experience or attachment to the company. Furthermore, while learning to value a company may itself at points feel mechanical, the act of putting these valuation tools into practice and investing, should be accessible and interesting, if not profitable!

Glossary

Angel investor – A high net worth individual who provides financial backing for very early-stage companies in exchange for a shareholding in the company.

Annual report – An audited record of a company's activities and performance over a 12-month period. Companies also commonly produce quarterly and semi-annual reports.

Amortisation – An accounting method for allocating the cost of an intangible asset over its useful life.

Asset class – Securities with similar features. The most common asset classes are stocks, bonds and derivatives.

Bull market – A bull market occurs when there is an extended period of rising stock prices. The opposite is a bear market, where there is an extended period of falling stock prices.

Beta – A measurement of volatility calculated as the covariance between the return of the company and the broader market, divided by the variance of the market. A reading of 1 is neutral, while above 1 means the company is more volatile, and less than 1 means the company is less volatile.

Blue chip – A well-established company that is considered high quality and relatively low risk.

Board – An elected group of individuals who represent shareholders and typically meet quarterly or semi-annually. The board should be involved in significant company decisions and ensure that management acts in the best interest of shareholders.

Bond – A bond acts like a loan but is far more easily traded – the distinction is similar to that between private equity and public equity.

Capital gain – When a profit has been made, this is the difference between the purchase price and selling price. The opposite is a capital loss.

Capital market – A market that matches those who have capital (money) with those who want it. It can be divided into the primary market, where shares are sold, and the secondary market, where those shares are then traded.

Capitalised cost – A cost that is recognised as an asset rather than being expensed in the period incurred. It is used when the benefits of an item – for example, production equipment – are expected to be derived over multiple periods.

Cash equivalent – Short-term money-market instrument that can be easily converted into cash – for example, treasury bills.

Chief executive officer (CEO) – The CEO is the highest-ranking executive in a company, and as such is the chief point of communication between the board and broader executive team. The responsibilities of the role include being a part of all major decisions, whether operational or strategic.

Cost of debt – The effective interest rate that a company pays on its debt (including both loans and bonds). This can be further broken down to the 'after-tax cost of debt' which takes into account the tax deductibility of debt.

Cost of equity – Otherwise known as the 'required return', the cost of equity is the minimum return a rational investor should require for an equity investment.

Common stock – Securities that represent ownership in a company.

Correlation – A statistic that measures the extent to which two securities move in relation to one another. A correlation of minus 1 would mean that the securities move in entirely opposing directions, whereas a correlation of 1 would mean that they moved entirely in tandem. A correlation of zero would suggest that there is no correlation at all.

Default – Failure of a debtor to make timely payments of interest and/or principal.

Depreciation – An accounting method of allocating the cost of a tangible asset over its useful life.

Discount rate – The required return used in a discounted cash flow valuation to determine the present value of future cash flows.

Diversification – A means of reducing risk by owning a variety of different investments to limit exposure to any single one.

EPS – Short for 'earnings per share', calculated as earnings divided by total shares outstanding.

Equities – Shares which are issued by a company and represent ownership in it. The equity market is referred to as the stock market, while an 'equity investor' is an individual or company that invests in that market.

GDP – Short for 'gross domestic product', GDP is the total monetary value of all finished goods and services produced within a country in a specific period. It is used as a measure of economic performance for a country.

Goodwill – An intangible asset that arises due to an acquisition when the price paid is greater than the net fair value of the target. This is not amortised, but is instead tested for impairment.

Index – An investment index that tracks the performance of the stock market or a subset of that market. This is achieved by the inclusion of most of the target market's companies. An index is what is typically referred to when commenting on a market's performance.

Inflation – A broad rise in the prices of goods and services.

Interest rate – The amount of money that an issuer of debt agrees to pay the holder of the debt. It is most often referenced as a percentage of the face value of the loan or bond issued.

IRR – Short for the 'internal rate of return', this is the discount rate that makes the net present value of all future cash flows zero. It is commonly used to assess private equity investments and projects. The higher the IRR, the more attractive the opportunity.

IPO – An initial public offering (IPO) refers to the process of a company selling shares in return for capital on a public exchange. Once issued, these shares can then trade in what is known as the secondary market.

Market capitalisation – The market value of a company. This is calculated as the price per share multiplied by the total number of shares outstanding.

Market price – The current share price of an asset at which it could be bought or sold.

Opportunity cost – The potential benefit an individual or company forgoes when choosing an alternative.

Preferred stock – There are a several types of preferred stock. Typically however, they are classified within equity, have a fixed dividend, are further up the capital structure than equity in the event of liquidation, and have no voting rights.

Public company – A company whose shares are listed and traded on a stock exchange, such as those of New York, London or Hong Kong.

Private company – A company that does not have its shares traded on a public exchange. Transactions in its shares are therefore more complex and far less frequent.

Quarter – There are four quarters in a year, each lasting three months. Many public companies are required to provide quarterly updates to the market.

Recession – A downturn in economic activity that is typically defined as two or more quarters of contraction in GDP.

Required return – The minimum acceptable level of return that a rational investor should expect to receive for an investment. This is based on a combination of the risk-free rate and the risk premium.

Risk-free rate – Assumed to be the effective interest rate on a 10-year government bond.

Risk premium – The return in excess of the risk-free rate that a rational investor should require for a risky investment.

Securities – Another name for investments such as stocks or bonds. The term derives from the name of the document that certifies an investor's ownership.

Share – A unit of ownership in a company.

Standard deviation – A statistical measure of volatility. It measures the amount of dispersion that a data set has around its mean. A low standard deviation would imply that the data points tend to be not far from the mean, while a high standard deviation would indicate that the data points are spread out further from the mean.

Stockholder – Otherwise known as a 'shareholder', a stockholder is the owner of a company's common or preferred stock ('shares').

Stock market – Otherwise known as the 'stock exchange', the stock market is where shares in a company can be issued and then traded. Major stock markets include those of New York, London and Hong Kong.

Total return – Typically a percentage figure, this is a measure of overall performance. For shares, it would include both the income return (dividends) and capital gain/loss (share price change).

Valuation – An estimate of the value or worth of a company's equity.

Weighted average cost of capital (WACC) – a figure that shows a firm's overall cost of capital. It includes proportional weightings for the cost of equity and the after-tax cost of debt.

Reading list

The following books in my view will have a profound effect on how you interpret events and evaluate investment, particularly with regards to learning from the past, rationalising the present, and thinking outside the box when predicting the future.

- *A Short History of Financial Euphoria* – John Kenneth Galbraith
- *Accounting for Growth* – Terry Smith
- *Crowd Funding: How to Raise Money and Make Money in the Crowd* – Modwenna Rees-Mogg
- *The Black Swan: The Impact of the Highly Improbable* – Nassim Nicholas Taleb
- *Antifragile: Things that Gain from Disorder* – Nassim Nicholas Taleb
- *The Ascent of Money: A Financial History of the World* – Niall Ferguson
- *The Liquidity Theory of Asset Prices* – Gordon Pepper & Michael Oliver
- *How the Mighty Fall: And Why Some Companies Never Give In* – Jim Collins
- *Blue Ocean Strategy* – Renée Mauborgne and W. Chan Kim
- *The Greatest Trade Ever* – Gregory Zuckerman

- *Black Box Thinking: The Surprising Truth About Success* – Matthew Syed
- *The Outsiders: Eight Unconventional CEOs and their Radically Rational Blueprint for Success* – William Thorndike
- *Misbehaving: The Making of Behavioral Economics* – Richard Thaler
- *Zero to One: Notes on Startups, or How to Build the Future* – Peter Thiel & Blake Masters

Made in the USA
Monee, IL
10 November 2026

0309ec20-2af6-444d-9dd6-0b6c7c5158a1R01